Being Successful in...

Patents, Copyright & Trade Marks

Peter Hanna

BLACKHALL
Publishing

This book was typeset by
Artwerk
for
BLACKHALL PUBLISHING
26 Eustace Street
Dublin 2
Ireland

e-mail: blackhall@tinet.ie

© Peter Hanna, 1999

ISBN: 1 901657 28 0

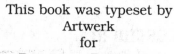

A catalogue record for this book is available
from the British Library.

Printed in Ireland by
Betaprint Ltd.

Series Foreword

*The Being Successful in...*series is a new series of practical books, which provide an accessible and user friendly approach to the common problems experienced by small to medium-sized, growing businesses.

The series will help businesses in the start-up phase but also covers problems encountered during the all-important development phase. They will be helpful to businesses which are starting to grow and which need to cope with a range of unfamiliar, difficult and often competing issues.

The books in the series are comprehensive and yet concise, and they treat the topics in question succinctly and without recourse to jargon. Practical examples, checklists and pointers on to further sources of help and advice are included to supplement the text.

Books published in the *Being Successful in..*series in early 1999:
Being Successful in...Report Writing
Being Successful in...Customer Care
Being Successful in...Presentations
Being Successful in...Time Management
Being Successful in...Budgeting

Forthcoming books in the series:
Being Successful in...Overcoming Stress
Being Successful in...Winning Business
Being Successful in...Business Planning
Being Successful in...Public Relations

I hope you find this book useful.
Veronica Canning
October 1998

This book is dedicated to the memory of
Gearoid O'Sullivan (1955-1996)

Contents

Acknowledgements

I would like to acknowledge the assistance of the series editor Ms Veronica Canning and Ms Ulrike Bubl for typing the manuscript.

Peter Hanna

Introduction

If you have a good idea, should you patent it? Maybe you should copyright it. Or would it be better just to trademark it? In fact, you can do none of the above. Well, how exactly do you protect a company's good *ideas*, its "intellectual capital"?

If you own a small business, or are a manager in a medium-sized firm, do you fully understand the role of patents, copyright and trade marks in your business or have you been affected by competitor's rights in this area? If you want to learn more about how "the system" works, what you can actually protect, how, when and why, then read on.

Patents, copyright and registered trade marks are legal rights that your company can acquire, but this is not a legal textbook. There are no references to Patents Acts or decided cases. You are a layman, not a lawyer, but often the lawyers and advisors can make the whole subject rather more difficult to understand than it needs to be.

Chapter 1

Understanding Patents, Copyright And Trade Marks

This chapter will help you to:

- understand "intellectual capital";
- realise the difference between patents and copyright;
- know to which advisors you can turn for help;
- know how to enforce your rights in this area.

Understanding Patents, Copyright And Trade Marks

> To apprehend thus, draws us a profit from all things we see.
>
> William Shakespeare, *Cymbeline*

This book is really about *understanding* patents, copyright and trade marks, the differences between them, when each is appropriate and what exactly they protect. These are known as intellectual property rights, but the more fundamental concept of *intellectual capital* will be examined and how important it is in today's knowledge-based economy to recognise, manage and protect these assets.

WORD TO THE WISE
Intellectual capital has to be recognised and valued and steps must be taken to protect it.

PROTECTING IDEAS

You cannot actually protect an idea or concept, as such, no matter how good or ingenious it is. The best way to protect it is to keep it secret – confidential to the people in your company. Once it has been put down on paper or recorded in some way, the expression of the idea can be protected by copyright. If that idea relates to the improvement of a design or the aesthetic qualities of a product, the design can be registered, or protected by design right (in the UK). If your idea or concept is truly novel and overcomes a technical problem and can be embodied in a man-made product or an industrial process, if it is an 'invention', then you could get a patent for that product or process. In all cases, the underlying concept or idea is essential, but it is not a thing that you can protect in the abstract sense; the law can only give protection to tangible things, such as the expression (copyright), the physical manifestation (design) or the industrial application (patent) of the idea or concept.

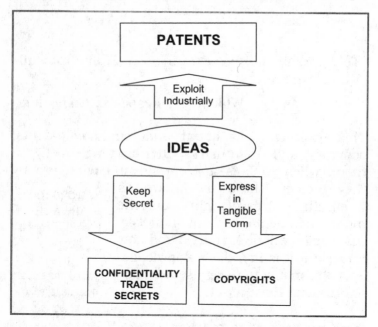

INTELLECTUAL CAPITAL

The good ideas that you own and the people in your company come up with every day (and that can be translated into competitive advantage and real profit) are your company's intellectual capital. It has to be recognised and valued by everyone in the company, and steps must be taken to protect it. Only copyright and design right (in the UK) are automatic. Patents, design registrations and trade mark registrations all require an examination and registration process and you are best advised to have a patent attorney or trade mark agent handle this for you.

Patents, registered designs and registered trade marks are treated as *intellectual property* and give your company valuable statutory monopoly rights.

(This is explained further in Chapter 2.)

DIFFERENCES BETWEEN PATENTS AND COPYRIGHT

A patent is the strongest and most respected type of intellectual property right and is the nearest you will get to protecting the basic or underlying concept. A single patent can cover the essential features of a product as well as very many close relations and alternatives, for example, a machine by which the product is made, the different processes by which it could be made, even the different uses to which it could be put.

The Patent Office grants a patent for an invention which it finds is an advance on the state of the art, not an obvious development, as judged by a Patent Examiner who has access to vast databases of technical literature and prior patents. No patent is ever granted with any guarantee of validity, and this can always be challenged by someone else who can prove that a patent should not have been granted. Patents can therefore be strong or weak. Nevertheless, a patent gives you a monopoly for a limited time, which may be up to twenty years.

Copyright arises automatically when a copyright 'work' is created or published. Most people mistakenly believe that it gives you some sort of monopoly like a patent, but it does not. It is a very narrow right that only gives protection against the work being copied in any form. It is relatively easy to get around, because ideas can be copied without copying the expression of the idea. (This is explained further in Chapters 5 and 7.)

PATENTS POLICY AND MANAGEMENT

Although the European Patent Office reported that

over 100,000 European patent applications had
been filed in 1997 (the biggest number yet in one
year with the chemical, pharmaceutical and manufacturing industries still owning the most patents) a
recent European survey commissioned by Derwent
Information for Information Research Network
showed that just under 20 per cent of the companies that responded said they had *never* filed any
patent applications.

The survey shows that, even though ever-
increasing use is being made of the patent system,
there is still a significant number of companies that
are outside the system. Of those who use the patent
system, 81 per cent have a patent policy. There still
appears to be an ad hoc approach in most companies to the process of identifying opportunities for
patenting their products. These opportunities can
most easily be identified by carrying out a technological audit on a regular basis.

However, while patents are seen as vital to future
development, half the senior managers say they do
not have a full understanding of how to manage
patents. (This area is considered further in
Chapters 3 and 8.)

ADVISORS AND ADVICE

There are many professionals to whom you must
turn for advice.

- A **patent attorney** will guide you through the
  process of patenting and obtain the strongest
  possible patents for you, and advise you on the
  scope of competitors' patents.

- A **trade mark agent** will, likewise, handle
  trade mark registrations and carry out searches when you are adopting a new brand name.

- A **licensing consultant** can identify patented
  technologies for inward licensing or locate part-

ners in other markets where you can license out your own patents and receive a royalty income.

- A **solicitor** can advise on employment contracts, agreements, licences, copyright and contentious issues.

The important thing in understanding patents, copyright and trade marks is when to seek advice. An invention *must* be kept secret before a patent application is filed. Searches *must* be carried out before the launch of a new branded product, to ensure freedom of use of a trade mark. Action *must* be taken promptly to enforce granted patents and registered trade marks and to stop infringers. (This is explained further in Chapter 4.)

THE PATENT SYSTEM

There is much about the patent system that is misunderstood. It goes back a long time and in some ways is paradoxical. How can a State-granted monopoly encourage competition, innovation and disclosure of ideas?

Most patents are granted for quite small improvements, they are rarely very wide in scope, blocking off the development of a whole industry. Patents are thought to encourage innovation by rewarding research and development effort, with a strictly defined monopoly for a limited time only, before an invention becomes public property. As part of the bargain, the State receives a full disclosure of the invention in the patent specification, without this disclosure a patent will not be granted.

Patent specifications are published and form a vast repository of technical knowledge. Much technical information, which would otherwise be lost or kept secret, will enter the public domain, undoubtedly to everyone's advantage. However, there is actually no empirical way of testing how effective a system of patent monopolies is, but the perception is widely held that the system must work. (This is explained further in Chapter 5.)

BRANDS AND TRADE MARKS

Brands have the potential to become the most important assets a company may own. They can live for a long time – the famous Michelin man was 100 years old in 1998! Brands consist of trade marks and trade marks can be words, symbols, logos or practically anything else with which customers will readily associate a company's goods and services.

Trade marks which are truly distinctive and which no one else has a legitimate right to use, such as sur-names and place names, can be registered and given monopoly rights. The great value of a registered trade mark is that it can be maintained in force *indefinitely*, by paying a renewal fee once every ten years. Patents still give relatively long protection, but expire after twenty years, and must be renewed annually. (This is explained further in Chapters 6 and 8.)

ENFORCEMENT

A patent is not an absolute monopoly; it is not an exclusive right to sell a product, because to do so might possibly infringe on other people's patents, designs and copyright. It is instead an exclusive right to stop others making, selling or importing products which fall within the scope of your patent.

It is a right which you must police and enforce yourself; no one will do this for you. Only a court can determine issues of infringement and validity of patents and litigation costs a lot of money. Very few cases ever go to full trial and this should be avoided whenever possible. (This is explained further in Chapter 9.)

REMEMBER

DO:

- Understand the fundamental differences between patents, trade marks and copyright; none of them protect ideas *as such.*
- Know what constitutes an invention and that not all inventions are patentable.
- Recognise the strengths of trade mark registration; a registered trade mark can be maintained in force *indefinitely,* patents and registered designs expire.
- Appreciate the value of *monopoly* protection afforded by patents, registered trade marks and designs.
- Value your professional advisors and follow their advice.

DO NOT:

- Let your company's good ideas – its *intellectual capital* – become public knowledge; be vigilant about maintaining secrecy.
- Put any product on the market without first investigating the possibility of patent protection, the strongest form of protection there is.
- Forget that maintaining your granted patents, registered trade marks and designs involves positive action, and renewal costs.
- Think of a patent monopoly as an exclusive right to sell a product; it is an exclusive right to stop others, and you have to enforce it against them.
- Ignore professional advice.

Chapter 2

Your Company Has "Intellectual Capital": How Should You Protect It?

This chapter will help you to:

- know what your intellectual property rights are;

- know what to do when you have a good idea;

- distinguish between the different types of protection available;

- ensure that you protect your intellectual property;

Your Company Has "Intellectual Capital": How Should You Protect It?

> Anything that won't sell, I don't want to invent.
> Thomas Edison

WHAT IS INTELLECTUAL CAPITAL?

Any company's balance sheet will show a value for fixed assets, creditors, etc. adding up to a book value. But the real value of many companies today, particularly technology rich companies, lies in the aggregate knowledge-base in the heads of people – its employees, past and present.

This is *intellectual capital*. The real capital of a software company, for example, is practically all intellectual capital. Increasingly, we are seeing knowledge-based industries, such as multimedia, where most of the raw materials are products of the human intellect alone. This intangible capital puts enormous value on a company as we can see when the book value is exceeded many times by its stock market value.

Intellectual capital is not just proprietary knowledge about a company's technical achievements and inventions. A very considerable human effort goes into designing new products, which may not be very innovative at all, but clever industrial design, and aesthetic appeal to the consumer, is what gives the product added value.

Good industrial design is not just of importance in consumer products; care should go into good design quality which will add value to industrial products, i.e. even where you might think the customer would be more influenced by functionality than aesthetics.

Intellectual capital is also measured by a companies intangible assets, in particular its brands; in many well-established companies, brand names and the added value they bring, are by far the most important assets. But small companies can build a brand with care and time; its value can rapidly be multiplied by, for example, building the brand into a franchise.

WHAT IS INTELLECTUAL PROPERTY?

You have intellectual capital. Your people have good ideas. You have developed innovative products and new brands. They are your company's intellectual property. Intellectual property can be protected, and you can and should take steps whenever possible to obtain the legal protection that is available. That is really the subject of this book. Intellectual property rights (known as "IPR") are statutory rights and are available in different forms.

> **WORD TO THE WISE**
> Legal protection is available for intellectual property – use it.

INTELLECTUAL PROPERTY RIGHTS

- Trade secrets and confidentiality.
- Copyright.
- Patents and utility models.
- Designs.
- Trade marks and service marks.
- Ancillary rights.

Basically, most intellectual property rights are there to protect ideas. There are four basic things you can do when you get a good idea.

FOUR BASIC THINGS TO DO WHEN YOU HAVE A GOOD IDEA

1. **Keep it secret.** You will be protected by the laws of trade secrecy and confidentiality.

2. **Write it down or record it.** You will be protected by the law of copyright.

3. **Embody it in an industrial application, a tangible product.** You may be able to obtain protection under law of patents, designs and ancillary rights.

4. **Exploit it commercially on the market as a brand.** You may be able to obtain protection under the law of trade marks and service marks.

1. Trade Secrets and Confidentiality

If you keep an idea secret or discuss it with work colleagues, you are protected by the law of trade secrets, confidentiality and contract law, but such laws may only give you a very limited amount of protection if you tell others outside your company.

Formulas may be protected in this way, for example, the fabled "secret ingredients" of *Coca-Cola*. This requires very rigid controls on confidential documents and information. Disclosing secret information to third parties under confidentiality agreements is fraught with danger. You must clearly state that a particular disclosure is confidential, and that no one else can be told without your prior, written approval.

Once out in the public domain, your idea is no longer secret and it will generally not be possible to obtain patent or design protection. Your rights under trade secret and confidentiality laws do not require registration – they are automatic. However, you have to prove they exist.

2. Copyright

If you write down or record your idea, whether on paper or electronically, then that expression of your idea becomes a "copyright work". Provided it is your original creation and you did not copy it from someone else, you are the author and the owner of that copyright.

This is an automatic right and it is free; it does not require registration. Copyright protects printed text, written material, books, brochures, advertising and packaging, graphics, artistic works, sound and film recordings, photographs, drawings, technical drawings, flowcharts, software source code listings, object code, multimedia, etc. All of these have one thing in common – they are expressions, in some tangible medium, of an idea.

Copyright does not, however, protect the basic ideas themselves. It merely gives protection against other people copying your particular expression of the idea. Copyright is not a monopoly, not an exclusive right. Another person can, independently, come up with exactly the same idea, express it in exactly the same way and they too can claim copyright. It is quite a narrow legal right, but it does protect the rights in the work as expressed by the copyright holder. (Chapter 7 explains copyright in more detail.)

3. Patents and Utility Models

If you embody your idea in some industrial application, be it a new process or a new product, then you may be able to obtain a patent. Patents offer the strongest form of intellectual property protection available, because they do protect the basic idea itself, provided that this represents an "invention". Only inventions can be patented.

An invention must relate to an industrial process or a product produced or used in industry or agriculture. It has to be "novel", i.e. not previously known or published anywhere. The degree of novelty can be very small indeed. It has to represent a real technical advance and solve a technical problem in a way that is not obvious – this is what it really takes to have a patentable invention. Many patents are granted for relatively small technical improvements.

You *must* keep your invention secret, and *not* put your product on sale, before you apply for a patent. Obtaining a patent (see Chapter 5) involves a registration process at the Patent Office and the use of a patent attorney. It takes time (maybe several years) and money (maybe many thousands of pounds) to obtain. A granted patent gives you exclusive rights – a monopoly – for a maximum term of twenty years.

You can enforce your patent against someone who says that they came up with the same idea independently of you. If it turns out that you were not the first person with this idea, your patent can collapse; a court can revoke it as being invalid. This does not happen very often, as courts tend to respect patents and the rights of patent holders, because patents in law are property.

A strong patent, and especially one that has withstood a challenge in court to its validity, is a very formidable weapon indeed. Chapters 8 and 9 will give some practical advice on how to exploit and enforce your company's patents.

A *utility model*, '*petty patent*' or *short-term patent* are nearly the same as a patent but are usually obtained more easily, quickly and inexpensively, and have a shorter term of protection. In Ireland the term is ten years. In the UK, this form of protection is not currently available.

4. Designs (Design Registration and UK Design Right)

Many new industrially produced products do not qualify for patent protection. A new bottle or container shape, pasta shape, striped toothpaste, wallpaper designs, airline seat configuration, even large-scale designs, such as the aeroplane itself, a ship's hull, car model, and the more truly aesthetic designs, such as jewellery or giftware, can all be protected by design registration.

Generally, original three-dimensional shapes are protected, however two-dimensional designs applied to articles such as crockery and repeating designs, such as on carpets, wallpapers or fabrics, are also protected. Textures and ornament with a distinctive design as applied to various articles can also in themselves be registered.

All of these have two things in common: originality and some recognisable aesthetic appeal to the customer. Originality means it has not been made and designed this way before, which is not necessarily the same as 'new'.

For example, you could register the design of a pen in the shape of a well-known bottle design. Design registration in this case is quite limited in the sense that you only get protection for the design, as it is applied to a specific article (the pen), not in the abstract sense, where it can be applied to anything which can be produced industrially. Also, while it is quite cheap, you may have to register many different designs separately, multiplying the cost significantly.

The important thing about design registration is that it is a monopoly right, and in this sense it is like a patent. If someone claims to have come up with exactly the same design, independently of you, they can be stopped. The term of protection varies from country to country, in Ireland a registered design lasts for up to fifteen years, in the UK up to 25 years. You must apply for design registration *before* the product has been offered for sale, and you apply to the Patent Office; it only takes a few months.

The design registration system is very effective, but it is not used to a very great extent. Moulded plastic products, such as containers, household goods and utensils are registered often, but clothing rarely. There are too many designs and they change too frequently. Purely functional designs for machine parts and very utilitarian products may not qualify because they lack any recognisable aesthetic qualities.

In the UK, it has been recognised for quite a long time that many companies are either unaware of the vast range of good designs which can be protected under the registration system, or find the whole registration system too cumbersome or expensive. In 1988, a whole new system of unregistered design rights was introduced. This has not replaced the existing registration system, but has strengthened the automatic copyright protection, which is available for three-dimensional designs, for a maximum of fifteen years. It has become a very effective system but only applies in the UK.

5. Trade Marks and Service Marks

Brands consist of trade marks. A trade mark is any name or symbol that denotes the goods or services of a particular trader and it can be protected by a relatively straightforward registration process.

All brands, corporate logos, trade marks, the whole make-up of a company's image (from its advertising, right down to the packaging and presentation of its products) have originated from intellectual creation on someone's part.

Creating, building and managing strong brands is an ongoing process, the very lifeblood of many companies, and it requires a very dedicated intellectual effort. The truly intangible thing about a successful brand is not just that it serves to identify your product, but that it operates on an almost emotional level, appealing to deep senses of your customers' satisfaction and loyalty.

The generation of intellectual capital and the real and potential value it adds to the company's balance sheet must be recognised. It may be hard to see at first, but every company is creating intellectual capital on technical, aesthetic and even emotional levels.

6. Ancillary Rights

Other specialised forms of intellectual property rights will be mentioned here in passing. They plug certain gaps and apply to certain sectors only.

- Plant varieties protection.
- Semiconductor chip protection.
- Supplementary protection certificates for patented pharmaceuticals and agrochemicals.

Plant Varieties Protection

Separate legislation gives protection for new varieties of nominated plants and their seeds. Plant varieties are excluded from patent protection, but cloning and genetic engineering techniques may be patented.

Semiconductor Chip Protection

Although deposited on a wafer of silicon, the microscopic features of circuitry on a semiconductor chip do have three dimensions. A special form of 'three-dimensional' copyright applies to semiconductor chip designs and the masks, or 'negatives', used in the photolithographic processes for making a semiconductor chip. This protection is for companies such as Intel.

Supplementary Protection Certificates

Since it can take as long as twelve years or more to bring a new patented pharmaceutical to the market, that will leave only eight years or less of useful life from a 20-year patent for the exploitation of the patent. Agrochemicals also have to undergo field trials, which may take years before marketing approval is allowed.

Within six months of marketing approval, or patent expiry, whichever is first, the pharmaceutical or agrochemical company can apply to the Patent Office for a Supplementary Protection Certificate (SPC) extending the useful patent life by up to five years. However, this extended protection is only given for specific patented products, which are on the market, not the whole range of products, which might come within the scope of the patent.

This concession is enough for the big pharmaceutical companies; it is nearly always in the last few years of the term of a patent where big profits are earned, before the generic manufacturers jump in.

CONCLUSION

The challenge facing companies today is in understanding and identifying the often huge differential between its balance sheet and its market valuation. This gap can only be accounted for by its intangible assets – what must be viewed as the core value of company, i.e. its intellectual capital. We should not be surprised when the hidden gold is revealed and the worth of an organisation is transformed, as we often are with acquisitions, mergers and flotations.

The small to medium-sized company must recognise that it has intellectual capital, that this can be measured, managed and nurtured to become a vehicle of growth. Most of all, it must be remembered that it can be protected.

REMEMBER

DO:

- Recognise your company's intellectual capital and how it adds real and potential value to the company's balance sheet.

- Impose rigid control on confidential information and documents within your company to maintain secrecy.

- Appreciate the differences between the different types of protection that you can obtain and that some of these (e.g. patents, registered designs and registered trade marks) are not automatic and require specific action to obtain.

- Think of intellectual capital as intellectual property; it belongs to your company and statutory protection is available.

- Keep good records of all your company's intellectual property and build a portfolio.

DO NOT:

- Think intangible aspects of intellectual capital cannot be valued (e.g. its brands) – they can, and can add significantly to a company's worth.

- Forget intellectual capital is mobile – employment contracts must include confidentiality clauses which endure after an employee has left to ensure they do not disclose information.

- Disclose details of inventions or designs to anyone outside your company, before a patent or design registration application has been made.

- Offer for sale or put on the market any product before getting advice as to whether patent or design protection is possible.

- Think that big brands are for big companies – a small company can build a brand, which, with care and time, can rapidly multiply its value through franchising.

Chapter 3

The Five Most Important Decisions You Must Make

This chapter will tell you:

- who should be responsible for managing intellectual capital;
- how to develop an intellectual capital policy;
- how to develop a strategy for protecting your intellectual capital;
- how to get timely and accurate advice;
- how to make best use of the technology information resources now available.

The Five Most Important Decisions You Must Make

> The price of greatness is responsibility.
>
> Winston Churchill

THE FIVE MOST IMPORTANT DECISIONS YOU MUST MAKE

The last chapter was an introduction to understanding what lies behind patents, copyright, trade marks and, on a deeper level, what is now termed intellectual capital. To leverage the power of your company's intellectual resources and turn these into an integral part of your company's business practice, you may need to re-think some traditional ideas and make decisions affecting the whole management of the company.

1. Who in your company will be responsible for managing its intellectual capital?

2. Decide on a policy.

3. Decide on a budget and a strategy.

4. Choose advisors, get advice, and at the right time.

5. How can your company best use the vast technology information resources that are now available?

1. WHO IN YOUR COMPANY WILL BE RESPONSIBLE FOR MANAGING ITS INTELLECTUAL CAPITAL?

Responsibility

Is anyone truly responsible already? The managing director of a small company often takes personal responsibility for patent programmes, trade mark registrations, and the problems caused by conflicts with other people's patents and trade marks. While the managing director must understand how intellectual capital can be protected and must obviously make strategic decisions, he or she does not have enough time for taking true responsibility.

Sometimes, the managing director has personally come up with many of the good ideas, which are to be protected or patented. They are his/her babies, which will not be handed over easily. Narrow focus of responsibility where the managing director attempts to cover all the issues, even in the smallest company, is not good.

Awareness

In fact, every single employee of your company should be educated in the importance attached to its intellectual resources, because every single employee has the potential to come up with those good ideas and create new intellectual capital for your company. The responsibility for managing intellectual capital in a general sense is really everyone's responsibility.

> **WORD TO THE WISE**
> Every employee of the company should be educated in the importance attached to its intellectual property.

The old-fashioned, passive approach of the 'suggestion box' has become a proactive, company-wide mission to *listen* to ideas, to improve, to innovate, to excel. There has to be awareness that even the smallest improvements can be protected, can add value. If a company is product-led, where only constant innovation will keep it ahead, there is no better way to get all employees involved in the process than to have an incentive scheme, an actual reward, for having their name as an inventor in a patent obtained by the company.

Budgets and Strategy are Interlinked

If your company is serious about developing and protecting its intellectual capital, in particular if you intend to build a portfolio of patents, even a relatively small one, it will cost money. The accountant or financial controller has to share responsibility and devise a budget.

Companies that devolve responsibility for patents and trade marks to its financial controller, often fall into a trap. Too much attention can be placed on the budget, the budget is drawn up too tightly, or (in Ireland) on tax advantages accruing from patents, and valuable patents can be allowed to lapse or not be renewed, because they are costing too much. Once allowed to die, a patent cannot normally be brought back to life. The longer term strategy is sacrificed to short-term expediency and, as will be explained, you do need a long-term strategy.

Do not get Lost in Technical Details

Some small to medium-sized companies delegate responsibility for particular patent programmes and innovative projects, which involve a number of patents, to the technical manager or project manager. This has the advantage that the patent attorney will have instant access to all the technical information needed to draw up a patent application. However, there are legal and business aspects to patenting that the technical manager may not fully understand. To be truly responsible for a company's intellectual capital, you have to be able to see the big picture and not get lost in detail.

Management Focus

It is not going to be suggested to whom in your company or at what level of management, ultimate responsibility for managing intellectual capital should rest; only that someone has to have it. It can be a frustrating experience as a patent attorney, to see some brilliant ideas wither on the vine, for simple lack of water. This is not because of a lack of money to develop innovative products and ideas, which of course can be the death of many, but of the lack of management time and focus devoted to nurturing and protecting these assets, once created.

In deciding who should have true responsibility in this area, whether it is an individual or a small team, the following attributes will be needed.

For managing intellectual capital, you need:

* vision;

* real understanding of the value of patents, trade marks and copyright;

* ability to plan and budget;

* a good enough understanding of the technology, and your competitors;

* knowing when, and where, to get advice, and what it costs.

2. DECIDE ON A POLICY

Start with your Mission Statement

You should look again at your company's mission statement. Does it in any way reflect the pride you take in your company's brands, its unique products, its attention to detail, design, in effect all the fruits of its intellectual capital? Does everyone in your company know that you have some very valuable assets that they may not see and to which, on any day of the week, they could be adding?

Build Awareness

You have to develop a policy on intellectual capital and everyone must know what it is. It must begin with an educational process and awareness-building. There is still a tremendous ignorance about the patent system, how copyright works and how brands are managed.

Respect Other People's Rights

Your policy must ensure that you and your employees respect other people's intellectual property rights. The penalties for copyright theft and infringement are severe and illegal copying of others products cannot be allowed. A frightening number of companies today have breached copyright in the software they are using and in information they can get 'free' from on-line sources, i.e. the internet. Teach your employees to respect other people's rights.

Intellectual Capital is Mobile

Employees come and go. They gain a lot of knowledge when they are in your employment and they are going to use it when they leave. Review your employment contracts and make absolutely sure they include confidentiality clauses and provide for information, which is your company's property, to remain confidential to that individual after they have left your employment.

Intellectual capital is mobile – it goes out of your office or factory every evening and comes back in again in the morning. Stealing company secrets happens all the time, so take precautions – have standard confidentiality agreements with contractors, dealers, consultants, not just full-time employees.

Standard Contracts and Agreements

Really what you need is an overall knowledge management policy, backed up with a code of practice which includes written agreements where necessary. Employment contracts are the correct place for a general agreement to assign all rights in intellectual property from the employee to the employer.

> **WORD TO THE WISE**
> Inventions made in the course of employment or a part of the normal duties of an employee or director of a company belong to the company.

Inventions made in the course of employment or as part of the normal duties of an employee or director of a company belong to the company. Nevertheless, a written assignment of rights is required and a separate one may be required every time patent rights in certain countries (e.g. the USA) and copyright in any work (e.g. written material, art work, designs, software) is acquired by the company. Your solicitor and patent attorney can advise on standard contracts and agreements and you must have a system for ensuring that these are signed and kept on file.

3. DECIDE ON A BUDGET AND A STRATEGY

Blanket Coverage is Unrealistic

If you have a budget for in-house research and development, for new product development, for branding and brand management, has the cost of acquiring patent protection and registering designs and trade marks been made a component of that budget? Obtaining patents is an especially expensive process, the registration of designs and trade marks less so. Only a few of the largest multinationals even contemplate 'worldwide' protection. Generally speaking, you have to apply for and maintain individual patents, designs and trade marks in each country and hence the rapid multiplication of costs.

A Realistic Strategy

Suppose you have a strategy for developing new products at intervals to replace those that are nearing the end of their product life cycle and that you have given your financial controller or product manager a budget to bring each new product to market. You may have a new line of products or an improved model of an existing design. You may be re-branding an existing product. It may be an innovative breakthrough that could change the fortunes of the entire company – something really hot. In every case it would be wise to consider carefully, just how much each new product is likely to add value, its true worth to the company, and then decide how much you would be prepared to set aside to protect that product, and the whole investment in time and money that you have put into its development. Consider the following.

BUDGETING CONSIDERATIONS

- What protection is available?
- What is it likely to cost?

What Protection is Available?

- Is there anything that is patentable? (See Chapter 5.)
- Do you have a new brand name? (See Chapter 6.)
- Can you fall back on copyright and designs? (See Chapter 7.)

What is it likely to Cost?

- Initial filing costs.
- Examination, grant and patent office fees.
- Renewal fees after grant.

A patent attorney can tell you exactly what these costs will be.

By deciding first of all what the appropriate type of protection is (patent, trade mark, copyright, design) or what combination of these is available and then what this will cost, you then have to decide on a sensible strategy of what countries will be covered, so as to come within your budget. Consider the following.

STRATEGY CONSIDERATIONS

- Who are my main competitors?
- Who is most likely to copy my new product?
- Where are my main markets?

Who are my Main Competitors? Who is most likely to Copy my New Product?

- You must know who your competiors are and where their manufacturing operations are located.
- You should know the source of similar, but inferior quality products, the counterfeits and the rip-offs.
- Which competitors are you most concerned about, the ones who are eating into your market share?

Where are my Main Markets?

- Not just now, but in five or ten years time.

Where to Patent?

In a patent programme, you should first of all cover those countries where your most important competing manufacturers are located. The next tier would be the countries where the smaller fry are located. Remember if you are ever going to enforce your patent, it is the manufacturers that you will sue for patent infringement.

The next tier would be the countries which might be important markets, but which might not have any significant competing manufacturers. For those countries, patent coverage would be less important because you could only really hope to enforce your patent against an importer or an individual customer, which is not as good as stopping production at source.

Finally the last tier would be the countries where the blatant copiers, counterfeiters and rip-off merchants are located. Patents can be obtained in most countries in the Far East, China, the countries of former Soviet Union, etc., but they will be very difficult to enforce. It is best to rely on customs regulations and anti-counterfeiting laws to stop this activity if it is a serious problem. In deciding on a budget for a patent programme, take a sensible and measured approach, getting the best value for money in terms of the coverage obtained.

The following is a list of the points you should consider (in order of importance), when deciding in which countries to file for patent protection.

1. Where there are big competing manufacturers?

2. Where there are smaller competing manufacturers?

3. Where there are important markets?

4. Where there are counterfeiters?

4. CHOOSE ADVISORS, GET ADVICE AND AT THE RIGHT TIME

Where to Find Advisors

Chapter 4 will explain the role of patent attorneys, trade mark agents, solicitors, accountants, tax advisors and licensing consultants. How they operate in their role as advisors to your company, how each can help you and when you should seek their advice.

You will need outside professional advice from different sources. The first advisor you will need is a patent attorney. Lists can be obtained from various sources (see the 'Further Resources' section at the end of this book). Patent attorneys must have a technical qualification in addition to a professional qualification in patent law; most firms have specialists in engineering, chemistry, biotechnology, electronics and computer software, so find one who is competent in your technical area. It is best to deal directly with an experienced partner and to build a long-term relationship.

Other Advisors

Most firms of patent attorneys will also handle trade mark registrations and have qualified trade mark agents; some of the bigger firms will have in-house solicitors to handle agreements, contracts and contentious legal matters. If you are involved in any type of litigation involving patents, trade marks, designs or copyright, you will also need the services of a solicitor or general law firm, and they must retain a barrister. For the valuation of intellectual property and the tax considerations from patent royalties under a licence, you will need the services of one of the larger accountancy firms (large enough to have a specialist in this area, and these specialists are quite rare).

A patent attorney is still going to be your key professional advisor and may be able to point you to other professional advisors when they are needed.

Professional Advice Costs Money

What is important to remember is that professional advice is a valuable commodity and you must be prepared to pay for it, just like any other commodity. Do not be afraid of asking about the cost at every stage of the process of getting advice.

- How much is this present consultation costing me?
- How much will this present assignment cost?

The cost will build up if you are not careful. Every meeting with your advisors must have a clear aim, so get the answers to your questions, come prepared and find out in advance what information and materials to bring with you. Avoid two meetings and follow-up meetings when you could have planned and achieved the same with one meeting. Time is money and you will be charged for your professional advisors' time.

The process of obtaining patents and trade mark registrations in several countries in relation to a particular new product may span over two or three years. Get projections of the likely costs at all stages for each one of your company's accounting years to aid your budget. Get a patent attorney to help you in determining your overall budget year on year for obtaining protection for your new product.

Get Advice Early

The importance of getting advice from a patent attorney as early as possible must be stressed. Right at the stage of the inception of a new product design or when several designs are under evaluation, talk to your patent attorney. Everything will be held in strict confidence.

He or she will be able to advise you as to whether or not there is any chance of obtaining a patent; whether it is likely to be a 'strong' or 'weak' patent, whether it might be necessary to apply for more than one patent, whether a patent might cover several, related products, whether it might be better to adopt some other approach in product design to make the product more 'protectable' by way of the patent system or even to 'design around' someone else's patent.

This last point is important – you may be well advised to discover sooner, rather than later, what other patents already exist which could scupper your whole project. Have a patent attorney do some preliminary novelty searches and infringement clearance searches (See Chapter 5) as early as possible, not a week before the new product launch.

Searches and the preparation of an initial patent application all take time, normally two to three weeks at least. Remember the patent application must be filed at the Patent Office before your product has been offered for sale, disclosed in public in any way or put on the market.

Likewise when choosing a new brand name, which in itself can be a difficult and time-consuming process, get a trade mark agent to do the necessary searches well in advance of your market launch. It can be disastrous to find that your chosen brand name will infringe on someone else's registered trade mark once your product is on sale. To be forced to change your product's brand name early in its life and after you have invested in promotion and advertising might very well be the end of that product's life.

Get Advice about Infringement Straight Away

If you receive a letter from a solicitor or a patent attorney drawing attention to a competitor's patent, or which may be any way threatening in tone, get advice immediately from your own patent attorney. Do not delay, because even a letter which 'draws attention' to someone else's patent may be the prelude to an infringement lawsuit.

If you have a patent, and you become aware of a competitor who is selling something similar to your patented product, regardless of whether their product is being sold for a higher price or is inferior in quality, tell your patent attorney anyway, even if it is not causing you too much concern. This competitor could be a problem in time, but your very delay in bringing an infringement action against him could prejudice your whole chance of winning your case and/or obtaining a remedy (monetary damages) for past infringements.

If you have copied, or almost copied, someone else's idea, get advice as soon as you can as to your possible liabilities.

5. HOW CAN YOUR COMPANY BEST USE THE VAST TECHNOLOGY INFORMATION RESOURCES THAT ARE NOW AVAILABLE?

Millions of Patents are Accessible

Many millions of patents have been granted since the modern patent system began over 100 years ago. All include a detailed technical description or specification normally illustrated by semi-technical drawings. These documents comprise a vast store of technical information and identify international competitors, the patent holders, in any given technical field. With more and more patent databases becoming fully accessible on the internet, anyone with access to a suitably equipped computer can search this information. (A list of some useful websites is given in the 'Further Resources' section at the end of this book.)

Database Searching

However, there are many pitfalls involved in searching the patent databases. Searching combinations of keywords is very hit and miss. The technical jargon used in different fields evolves and, of course, US and European jargon varies. However, the World Intellectual Property Office (WIPO), a UN organisation, has developed an elaborate classification system for inventions, the International Patent Classification system (IPC). By combining the most relevant IPC codes, you can home-in on the right technical area first, then highlight further relevant material by using keywords.

It is easy enough to learn the basics, but there are specialist searchers, and patent attorneys, who can probably unearth some very useful information for you at relatively little cost. Some of the best patent databases are subscriber only, e.g. Dewent's World Patent Index, covering English abstracts of virtually all patents which have been published in the last 30 years. This can be accessed via the big subscriber database hosts such as DIALOG and ORBIT-QUES-TEL. Apart from patent databases, these include access to hundreds of other databases including trade marks, business, medical, earth science, biotechnology, materials science, etc. – even a database of databases. You pay as you use, some databases being more expensive than others. The database hosts provide training but one or two sessions will get you going. Information gathering is a task best delegated to an intelligent and curious mind.

The Internet

What is really exciting about the growth of the internet for small to medium-sized companies is the amount of patent information that has only very recently become available in full text, and which is free. Since July 1998, the European Patent Office has made available the full text of all European Patents at www.european-patent-office.org. In early 1999, the US Patent and Trademark Office put the full text of all US patents at www.uspto.org. Within minutes, you can be looking at copies of other people's patents, right at your own desk, at next to no cost. It used to take a few days and cost up to about £10 to obtain a copy of one patent document.

Secrecy Window – Unpublished 'Patents Pending'

With the exception of the USA, the Patent Offices of all countries publish the contents of patent applications, within eighteen months of the date of the basic patent application being filed. There is therefore a period during which any patent application remains secret, so if a competitor has brought out a new product which says 'patent pending' within the last eighteen months, or claims recently to have developed a new 'patented' technology, you may not be able to see his patent application or even trace it. This 'secrecy window' is even more of a problem if you are investigating an US 'patent pending' because US patents are only published when the US patent is granted, which takes on average about 28 months from the US filing date.

Chapter 5 explains in more detail the art of searching and finding other people's patents. It explains about the following types of searches and how you could use them to your advantage.

- State of the art and technical information.
- Novelty.
- Infringement clearance.
- Validity.
- Watching.
- Current awareness.
- Subsequent art.
- Document search.

REMEMBER

DO:

- Decide who in your company will have true responsibility for managing intellectual capital.

- Have a written policy, a code of practice for employees, and standard contracts, covering your company's intellectual capital.

- Set aside a budget and have a strategy for protecting your company with patents, trade marks and designs.

- Know to whom you should go for advice and choose your professional advisors well.

- Know how to use the vast technology information resources provided by patent documents.

DO NOT:

- Have an ad hoc approach to your company's intellectual capital, it is too valuable.

- Forget about other people's intellectual property in your company policy – make sure employees respect other people's copyright.

- Attempt to obtain blanket coverage with a patenting programme, instead make strategic decisions about which countries are the most important.

- Tell a patent attorney to prepare a patent application within days of a shipment or product launch; there won't be enough time to do this properly and a lot of money could be wasted.

- Forget that patent documents are publicly available, can be searched and are the best information resource on competitor's technologies and the state of the art.

Chapter 4

Your Advisors: How They Can Help And Who To Avoid

This chapter will help you to:

- gain a better understanding of the role of your patent attorney, trade mark agent, solicitor, tax advisor and licensing consultant;

- understand how all these outside professional advisors can help you and your company develop, clarify and manage your policy and strategy for protecting your very valuable intellectual capital;

- recognise a few of the somewhat dubious or phoney service providers and to treat them with suspicion.

Your Advisors: How They Can Help And Who To Avoid

> A professional is a person who tells you what you know already, but in a way you cannot understand.
>
> Anonymous

THE ROLE OF THE PATENT ATTORNEY

Intellectual Property Audit

You should approach your patent attorney for general advice from time to time to identify how new products under development can best be protected and to help you with your company's strategy and budget planning.

A very good idea is to have your patent attorney spend time on site to carry out an 'intellectual property audit' whereby your patent attorney is shown everything you are doing now, all your product development plans and told about ideas that are still in your head. You will then have a full appraisal of the ways in which you have already built intellectual capital as well as how you can increase these assets with a realistic programme of patent, design and copyright protection.

There may be some hidden gold. You may have developed a much more efficient manufacturing process or one that overcomes a tricky technical problem. A process can be patented. Generally, you will have kept this secret, so you will not have forfeited the chance of obtaining a patent on your process.

General Advice

Your patent attorney should be called on regularly to give general advice as to whether or not ideas you want to exploit involve anything which might be patentable. Bring your patent attorney in at an early stage and well before any product launch, client demonstration, public exhibition, anything that would amount to a public disclosure of the new product.

Drawing Up the Patent Application

While it is not strictly necessary to engage a patent attorney to prepare and file a patent application, a patent is a legal document and if you want to enforce it against someone else, its scope and validity will have to be determined by a court. It is best to leave the drafting of a patent application to a professional. Even if you feel familiar with the patenting process and so wish to attempt to do this yourself, the drawing up of an application is fraught with pitfalls. The most important part of any patent application is the patent specification.

A patent attorney is trained to draw up the patent specification according to the legal requirements, which are as follows.

REQUIREMENTS AND ELEMENTS OF A PATENT

- **Technical field and background art.** To present a clear description of the relevant technical field of the invention and the relevant background (prior art) leading up to it.

- **Prior art problems and the technical solution of the invention.** To identify the problems associated with the nearest prior art, the technical solution, which the invention brings to the state of the art and the advantages, which would not have been obvious to someone skilled in the relevant technical field. This is what patent attorneys call the 'inventive step'.

- **Essential features of the invention.** To identify the truly essential features of the invention in very general terms.

- **Technical description of examples, embodiments of the invention.** To give a clear technical description of at least one way in which the invention can be realised. Many practical examples or 'embodiments' may be given which are aimed at a notional skilled reader, but the function of every nut and bolt does not have to be described. Nevertheless, a patent can be thrown out by a court as invalid if its technical description is insufficient. This is why you should choose a patent attorney who is competent in your area of the technology.

- **Patent claims.** This is where patent attorneys slip into some fairly arcane language, but it is crucially important to choose just the right words to define the scope of an invention. This is the legal part of a patent specification, found in a list of 'claims', and it is where the drafting skills of the patent attorney will become most apparent.

- **Drawings.** To have some illustration of all the embodiments which are described and covered by the claims. Patent drawings are not to be equated with engineering/technical quality drawings, but must show how everything works and interacts. They are rather quaint line drawings.

Strict Confidentiality

First and foremost then, the role of the patent attorney is to prepare, draft and file your patent application at the Patent Office. In your initial consultation with your patent attorney, there is often a fear of discussing too much detail – this after all is probably the first person outside your company to whom you will disclose your new idea. Rest assured that your patent attorney owes you a legal duty of strict confidentiality, and what you tell him or her will be privileged in law and will not amount to a premature disclosure.

Premature Disclosure may mean no Patent at all

The most common error made is that of prematurely disclosing an invention or design and then later seeking to apply for a patent or design registration. It is then too late! *Never* discuss any invention or design you wish to exploit commercially with *anyone* who is not under a legal obligation of confidentiality.

A premature disclosure, written or oral, to just one such person, which can later be proven, will invalidate any patent or design registration which you might obtain. From the day your patent attorney files your patent or design application at the Patent Office, you are then free to disclose. Up to that point it must be kept secret.

SECURING THE BEST POSSIBLE PATENT SCOPE

Patent Pending: Official Search

Once a patent application has been filed, an official search in the relevant art is carried out by the Patent Office. Your patent attorney will be able to fully assess the results of the Official Search Report and, if any unexpected published literature or previously granted patent turns up which describes anything close to your invention, your patent application may have to be amended and narrowed down in scope to steer clear of what is already known.

You cannot add any new subject matter into your patent application once it has been filed. You are stuck with what was included in the patent specification. Whenever your patent attorney amends this during the 'patent pending' process, he has to take great care not to include any limitations on the scope of the patent claims which are not absolutely necessary.

No Unnecessary Limitations

Similarly, a well-drafted patent specification must be broadly worded to cover the general inventive concept or principle, so that later product variations and modifications will still be covered by the patent. The patent attorney must play devil's advocate, and ask: "What would a competitor do to get around this?" Expect your patent attorney to ask probing questions. The object is to get you the strongest, broadest patent coverage possible. There should never be any unnecessary limitations in your patent.

Patent Pending: Examination

After the Official Search Report has been assessed, there is the following procedure of the official examination by the Patent Office. This is carried out by an extremely well qualified Patent Examiner. He or she will study the application in detail and the relevance of the prior art 'cited' in the Official Search Report.

The Examiner decides whether the three main criteria for granting a patent have been met: novelty, inventive step and industrial applicability. Maybe the Examiner will not discern anything novel and/or inventive in your application. Your patent attorney will have to use all his or her skill to overcome such objections, which are not uncommon. It is normally a process of negotiation and amending and re-amending but at all stages the client is kept informed and may even be involved if submissions are needed to explain the technical advance or the commercial success of the product.

In the difficult cases, your patent attorney may hold a face to face interview with the Patent Examiner to negotiate the granting of the patent and get the best possible scope of protection. In the rare cases where the Patent Examiner finally concludes that a patent must be refused, your patent attorney can argue your case at an appeal.

YOUR REPRESENTATIVE IN CONTENTIOUS SITUATIONS

Threatening Letters

Your patent attorney will be called on to represent your interests when you are at the receiving end of a threatening letter, threatening court proceedings under someone else's patent or if you wish to scare off an infringing competitor with your patent. (This is dealt with in more detail in Chapter 9.)

Oppositions

A European patent, once granted, may be opposed by a third party. This is done by the third party lodging an opposition at the European Patent Office at any time within nine months from the granting of the patent. You may wish to challenge the validity of a competitor's recently granted European patent by lodging your own opposition.

Your patent attorney should be qualified as a European patent attorney (EPA) and may represent you as opponent or respondent in these quasi-legal proceedings. About 6 per cent of all European patents granted are opposed. It is a much cheaper way of knocking out someone else's patent than mounting a challenge in court.

Legal Advice

If you get ensnared in any court proceedings involving a patent, your patent attorney can guide you as to your liabilities, strategies and outcomes. He or she can only act as your advocate in the British County Court, otherwise court proceedings mean retaining a solicitor and a barrister, but it is the role of the patent attorney to brief them on all aspects of the patent in question and on the law of patents.

THE ROLE OF THE TRADE MARK AGENT

Dual Roles: Patent Attorneys and Solicitors may be Trade Mark Agents

Nearly all patent attorneys are also qualified as trade mark agents, but most firms of patent attorneys will have specialist trade mark agents, who might also have additional legal qualifications. Solicitors are entitled to obtain the qualification of registered trade mark agent, and some firms of solicitors offer trade mark registration amongst their services.

Application for Registration

The process of applying to the Trade Mark Registry (in Ireland and the UK, a section of the Patent Office) may seem like it should be a straightforward process. However, it requires great care to get it right. In applying to register your brand name or logo as a trade mark, you have to specify the goods or services you are offering or intend to offer, under this brand. This is the goods/services specification, and it forms a part of your application. If it is too narrow, it will not give you the full protection you need for all your products/services; if it is too broad, your registered trade mark will be open to challenge and may be invalidated.

> **WORD TO THE WISE**
> You must not choose a prospective brand name that is the same as, or may be confused with, a brand name that is already registered or is 'pending' for the same goods services.

Your trade mark agent therefore needs to have a very good grasp of all your business activities and how these are likely to develop. He or she needs a very good feel for all the latest market trends and fashions and to have a knowledge of the rapidly changing hi-tech end of the market.

While it may be possible to secure a registered trade mark in respect of 'all computer hardware and software', a small company that is not yet well known in the computer business, or with only one or two actual products on offer so far, may have to be much more specific.

Why Trade Mark Searches are Necessary

The first point of contact you will have with your trade mark agent should always be for general advice as to whether or not a particular proposed brand name is possible to register. Some are not. For example, place names, personal names, words that directly or indirectly describe the product or service itself, are not considered distinctive enough and will probably be refused registration.

Most importantly, you must not choose a prospective brand name that is the same, or could even be confused with, a name that has already been registered or is 'pending' for the goods and services. Therefore, it is absolutely essential to get your trade mark agent to carry out some clearance searches to determine what other similar marks have been registered.

Even if it is decided not to register or if you still wish to go ahead and adopt a mark which is inherently unregisterable, you should have a 'freedom to use' search carried out. This should attempt to cover all brand names in use, although this is not always possible. Common law rights can be acquired over time in a brand name that has acquired a reputation and is well known, even if it was never registered as a trade mark.

Searches are a very important part of the trade mark agent's role. Once you have adopted a brand, or if you are responsible for managing a valuable and well-known brand, your trade mark agent can be given a 'watching search' brief, so that you will be informed of any applications to register a similar trade mark. You might be able to take simple action to prevent anyone else from succeeding in registering similar trade marks, even in different countries, which could ultimately dilute your brand. (Brand management is discussed further in Chapter 6.)

THE ROLE OF YOUR SOLICITOR

You will have a company solicitor or use a firm of solicitors and you will consult with them for general legal advice. It is generally only the larger firms, which will have specialists, or departments dedicated to intellectual property matters.

In the context of this book, the following things will fall within the role of your solicitor.

- **Employment contracts** and ensuring these have adequate provisions concerning ownership of inventions made in the course of employment and written assignment to the company when required. Clauses on confidentiality and restrictions on unauthorised disclosure even when the employee leaves employment.

- **Agreements** including licensing agreements, joint venture agreements, franchising agreements, collaborative research agreements with third-level educational establishments.

- **The law of trade secrets**, confidentiality and breach of confidence.

- **Contract law** and the enforceability of contracts entered into.

- **Copyright law** in general areas such as publishing, film making, sound recording, broadcasting and criminal actions to prevent piracy and copyright theft.

- **Product liability** and marking and labelling requirements for consumer products.

- **European law and competition rules**, as these affect licensing arrangements under patents, trade marks and copyright.

THE ROLE OF YOUR TAX ADVISOR

Tax and Patents: Ireland

In Ireland, there are opportunities to avail of tax relief if your company has obtained a patent; these are when the patented invention has been developed in Ireland, relates to manufacturing activity and your company is resident in Ireland for tax purposes. The tax relief relates to patent royalty income, i.e. there must be a licence in place between two legal entities (e.g. your trading company and a patent holding company).

However, the provisions under Irish tax law have become complex and specialist tax advice is required to take best advantage of these possibilities. It is the role of your patent attorney or solicitor to draw up the patent licence agreement.

General Tax Advice: International Licensing

If you are successful in licensing out your patented technology to a foreign company, the payment of royalties could involve some fairly complex tax questions including withholding tax and double taxation. In short, you will need advice from a tax expert if you are involved in international licensing.

THE ROLE OF YOUR LICENSING CONSULTANT

A Specialised Advisor

For the small to medium-sized company, the best way to exploit a patented product with considerable international market potential, or a patented process/technology that could be exploited in other countries, is to seek prospective licensees or joint venture partners in other countries where you have obtained patents. But how do you find time to identify these prospects and find the right partners, who could provide a royalty income stream for you? Your patent attorney will obtain your patents, but generally will not be able to assist you in exploiting your patents to their full extent by identifying possible licensees. Government agencies involved in industrial development and export trade may be able to assist you, but a specialised licensing consultant may be your best bet. (See 'Further Resources' at the end of this book.)

What a Licensing Consultant does

A licensing consultant will undertake a search to locate licensing partners, help you negotiate terms and set up the whole deal. He or she will charge a straight fee and not take a cut out of future royalties.

You may have to bring in someone else's patented technology and this is a strategy well worth considering. The 'its no good, it hasn't been invented here' syndrome is widespread, but if you add up the real cost of even hiring product designers and project consultants, it could cost a lot less and get you to market much faster, to 'license in' products and technologies from outside.

You will pay a downpayment and a continuing royalty and therefore there will be some cost, but this should be compared against the in-house research and development cost. Your licensing consultant will help you identify these opportunities and cost them for you.

SOME ADVISORS YOU MIGHT AVOID

Invention Brokers

Anyone may set up as an invention or exploitation broker with no specialist knowledge of patents. They generally attract the small or individual inventor, extract quite a large downpayment, and then set about sourcing a company, which may take up and commercialise the new invention.

There is a lot of upbeat literature and promises, but absolutely no guarantee of success. If they are successful in their search, the poor inventor will find that he has signed away 50-80 per cent of future royalties to the invention broker. Really it is not so difficult to source a prospective licensee, if the invention is truly worthwhile. For the small company, steer clear of invention brokers, pay the same, or a little more, and retain a reputable licensing consultant.

Data Miners

As mentioned before, the contents of nearly all pending patent applications are published at eighteen months from the basic filing date. This information very rapidly finds its way onto computer databases. Data miners sift this information and then try to sell it to people identified as fish who might bite the bait.

The bait is normally a computer-printed postcard or letter, telling you for example that your patent has been cited against someone else's subsequent patent application. You will not be given the details, but for a small fee you will receive them. This could be quite useful information, but you can do the mining yourself, at much less cost, by setting up a 'subsequent art search'. (This is explained further in Chapter 5.)

Copyright Banks

Copyright is an automatic right and you do not have to record your rights by lodging copies of the copyright work at the Patent Office or anywhere else. The USA has a registration system but it is not compulsory. Many people become concerned about proving a date of creation of written materials, computer source codes, technical drawings and other copyright works. You may have heard that the answer is to lodge the signed and dated material in a bank, with your solicitor or simply mailing the whole lot to yourself by registered post and keeping it unopened.

Recently, commercial operations styled as copyright banks will offer this service and record this date of creation and its proof for you, the author of the copyright work, for a fee of course. All of this has no validity in law and is in most cases quite unnecessary. The essential thing in copyright litigation is to prove that copying has taken place, that the other party's work is not original. If the other party can prove that he created his work independently, there is no copyright infringement. The actual date of creation is rarely an issue.

Fraudulent Trade Mark Registers

If you have a registered trade mark, and you receive an unsolicited offer from any commercial company to include your trade mark on their register, which may even look very official or international in character – beware! This is a complete fraud, but every so often the fraudsters pop up. The only way to obtain any legal rights is to register a trade mark officially. Official trade mark registers are only kept by the Patent Office.

REMEMBER

DO:

- Maintain regular contact with your patent attorney and have a regular intellectual property audit of your company to identify patenting opportunities.

- Give your patent attorney all the technical information he/she needs; anything less than a full and complete disclosure of an invention can jeopardise the patent.

- Get your trade mark agent to carry out clearance and freedom to use searches before adopting any new trade mark.

- Appoint a company solicitor to prepare and review all agreements and contracts.

- Employ a licensing consultant to help you exploit the full potential of a patented product or process; whether your own, by licensing out manufacture, or licensing in someone else's technology.

DO NOT:

- Regard your professional advisors as being there to solve your problems; instead seek advice when you don't have any problems and find how regular contacts will help you.

- Disclose any invention or designs to be exploited commercially with anyone who is not obliged to keep it confidential, *before* you get advice about patent or design protection.

- Let anyone else get away with attempting to register a similar trade mark to your own; instead give your trade mark a watching brief to alert you to this.

- Attempt to draw up any legal agreements without your solicitor's advice.

- Employ an invention broker to help you exploit a patented invention, they will seek a large cut from any future royalties.

Chapter 5

Playing The Patent System To Your Advantage

This chapter will help you to:

- understand the patent system;
- understand what can and cannot be patented;
- differentiate between the systems in Britain, Ireland, the EU and the US.

Playing The Patent System To Your Advantage

> The patent system...added the fuel of interest to the fire of genius in the discovery and production of new and useful things.
>
> Abraham Lincoln, 1859

THE PATENT SYSTEM – HOW IT WORKS

History

The patent system goes back hundreds of years. British monarchs were for a long time in the habit of granting special monopolies (letters patent) to all manner of deserving subjects from royal creditors to royal favourites. The arbitrary nature of this was of course unjust and in 1623 a Statute of Monopolies was enacted by a somewhat reluctant James I. The idea was as follows.

> When any man by his own charge and industry, or his own wit or invention doth bring any new trade into the realm, or any engine tending to the furtherance of a trade that was never before; and that for the good of the realm; that in such cases the King may grant to him a monopoly-patent for some reasonable time, until the subjects may learn the same, in consideration of the good that he doth bring by his invention to the commonwealth, otherwise not.
>
> English lawyer, arguing for a fair system of patents, 1602

The cornerstones of the British patent system, the first true patent system, were the same then as they are today – that anyone can apply for a patent, that there must be a 'new invention', that a state-endorsed monopoly is granted, that details of the invention are published and the patent is for a limited time period only.

It is remarkable that the principles of such a system have endured, through all the political changes, economic upheavals and the industrial and information revolutions that have occurred. Practically every country in the world today has a patent system – even China and closed economies such as North Korea.

Does the Patent System Work?

The value of the patent system has nevertheless been questioned – do monopolies not actually hinder technological development, does the territorial nature of a patent not hinder free trade, is the cost of the monumental bureaucracy (Patent Offices) justifiable? The prospect of a monopoly is certainly a simple incentive to invent and to disclose inventions, which will clearly benefit others working in the same area.

Within trading blocs, such as the European Union, national monopolies appear to go against the concept of a single market, but a single Community patent may soon overcome that. The cost of patenting has caused concern internationally, but much can and will be done to make the system more cost-efficient in future. A working group of experts, including some from the UK, the Chartered Institute of Patent Agents in the UK and the American Intellectual Property Law Association, convened in 1997 and they envisage a single, truly 'international patent' by the year 2020.

Will the System ever Change?

Over the years, there have been frequent attempts to change and perfect the 'system', but in reality there is little in the way of clear evidence to show how well the system works, or why...just a general presumption that it *does* work.

With the global system of patenting now so well in place, that would explain why it has been left pretty much alone for so long. Patents, their creation, avoidance, licensing and litigation, are mother's milk to the world of corporate technology and that is just the way the game is played.

> **WORD TO THE WISE**
> A patent application can take many years to go through a rigorous search and examination process, in many Patent Offices around the world.

Responding to Change

A patent application can take many years to go through a rigorous search and examination process in many of the Patent Offices around the world. The system is slow and cumbersome, but has been under pressure in recent years to adapt to the needs of its users in the fast-moving technologies of today.

In the past, the pharmaceutical industry has been the mainstay of the patent system, but as it generally takes well over five years to bring a new pharmaceutical to market, it did not matter if it took five years to get patents granted. Now Patent Offices have new 'fast track' procedures, which still take up to a year to obtain grant and the 'slow track' for those content to wait.

WHAT CAN BE PATENTED?

Only Inventions can be Patented: but what is an Invention?

First you must have 'an invention', but how do you know what that is? Strangely, the patent laws of many countries do not attempt to define the word 'invention'. It is difficult to draw a line between the mundane improvement, which anyone who set their mind to it could have thought of, and that clever inspiration, which few experience.

An invention has, first of all, to be new or 'novel', and that means it cannot have been published anywhere, or made available, or known to the public in any medium, by you, your company or anyone else, anywhere. This sounds like a pretty tough hurdle to cross, but it is not. Only a very small amount of novelty is required; in fact, if *exactly* the same thing has not been done before, your invention is novel. But that would make it too easy.

Next you must be able to show that 'clever inspiration' factor. Nearly always, someone has been there before you with something similar, but not exactly the same. To be patentable, your invention must not be just an obvious development on what has been done before. Your invention must solve a technical problem, with a clear technical or economic advantage to be gained, and it must represent, a genuine step forwards or an 'inventive step'.

As well as being novel and non-obvious, to qualify for a patent, an invention has to relate to the application of a technology (as explained in Chapter 2) and there are certain things, which may just not be patentable. These include the areas listed below.

WHAT CANNOT BE PATENTED	WHAT MAY BE PATENTED
• Discoveries, naturally occurring substances, laws of nature.	• Natural gene sequences, natural substances produced synthetically.
• Mere presentations of information; the expression of which is anyway covered by copyright.	• Scratch cards, easy to fold maps, carriers of information.
• Schemes, rules and methods of playing a game.	• Software for such, computer game consoles and board games.
• Methods of doing business, including pure business services as such.	• These can be patented in the USA, in Europe patents may be granted for electronic share trading, computer networking, some financial applications software.
• Methods for diagnosis, therapy or surgery.	• These can be patented in the USA, in Europe patents are limited to products used in such methods.
• Animal and plant life.	• Genetically engineered life forms and cloning methods may be patentable, a subject of much debate.

WHAT YOUR PATENT ATTORNEY NEEDS TO KNOW

What have you Invented?

Generally speaking you need professional advice from a patent attorney just to find out whether your invention can be patented. It actually takes very little to invent something, which may then be patentable. The majority of patents are granted for small improvements, often arrived at by good old trial and error. As Thomas Edison, one of the most famous inventors, put it, *"10 per cent inspiration and 90 per cent perspiration"*. An earth-shattering or ground-breaking innovation is not required.

Is it really an Invention?

Your patent attorney will need to know why you think the idea is clever, what are the technical advantages you perceive, what problem you have overcome. He needs to include this and as much relevant information as he can on the present state of the art in your patent specification, an essential part of your patent application, because he will need this if he has to argue with the Patent Office that your invention is not obvious.

Remember, even though you may think you know all about the competition, and have taken the precaution of having some searches done to identify prior patents, the Patent Office will do its own search and will nearly always uncover some relevant 'prior art' document which nobody knew about. If you have not given your patent attorney all the information he needs on the background to your invention, the solutions to the problem you have identified and the real advantages gained, he could have a hard time overcoming this very common objection, i.e. that your invention is obvious.

Disclose all Technical Information

You must give all the technical information, drawings, prototypes, etc. that are available and let the inventors or your technical manager, talk to the patent attorney. Get him to visit your plant or factory.

> **WORD TO THE WISE**
> Drawing up your own patent application and filing it yourself will not save money. Use a patent attorney.

A full technical disclosure is required to make a patent application or just to do a good search beforehand. You cannot hold something back or keep some secrets; your patent attorney is required to describe examples of the *best* method known to you of putting your invention into effect. There is a strict requirement about this in the USA. You could also risk losing your patent if you do not disclose *all* the prior art documents you know about to the US Patent and Trademark Office.

WHAT IS INVOLVED IN FILING A PATENT APPLICATION?

Let a Patent Attorney Handle it

Drawing up your own patent application and filing it yourself, is not a way of saving money. Engage a patent attorney. Pay his or her fee. The patent attorney will draw up that essential part of a patent application, the patent specification, with skill and technical expertise. This is a semi-technical, semi-legal document. It includes a discussion of the known state of the art, the contribution made by the invention, enough technical examples or 'embodiments' of how the invention is put into effect, illustrative drawings, and ends with the patent claims.

The patent claims are in many ways the most important part because it is the words of the claims, written in a prosaic, seemingly unintelligible language called patentese, which precisely define the scope of protection.

After you have given your patent attorney the information required, give him or her time to draft your application: a couple of weeks, not days. Hold up the first shipment or the market launch if necessary. The shortcomings of a hastily drawn-up application, with an insufficient disclosure, will come back later to haunt you, and could even result in your application being refused or your patent being found invalid.

THE 12-MONTH DEADLINE FOR FURTHER PATENT APPLICATIONS

Bring in your patent attorney at an early stage. If the product requires more development, but you are afraid the competition will beat you to the market, it may be possible to file an initial patent application, then one or more follow-up applications each with more technical disclosure, which can be tied together at the end of a 12-month period.

There are different strategies depending upon how close the product is to being launched. That 12-month period from your first patent application is also the deadline for extending it to other countries which is very, very expensive – filing your initial patent application before you need to can place a strain on your budget. Get costings of the different options and strategies so you know what you are letting yourself in for.

Novelty Searching

It may be advisable to have a search of prior patents carried out beforehand to get an idea what obstacles will lie in the way of a patent being granted to you. This is known as a novelty search and can be carried out for a few hundred pounds by a professional search company or a patent attorney.

The wheel has been invented countless numbers of times. It can save you many thousands of pounds in a fruitless patent filing programme, if you do locate a patent or literature reference describing exactly what you have invented. Even if the official searches carried out by the Patent Office do not find it, its very existence will mean that any patent granted to you will be invalid and built on foundations of sand.

However, in some cases, where the technology is in its infancy for example, novelty searches can be expected to reveal next to nothing, so you may as well press ahead with your patent application and wait to see what the Patent Office manages to find in its official search.

Do not File too soon: but do not Dither

The important thing is not to dither, it being essential to file your patent application *before* anyone outside your company knows about the invention and well before it has been put on the market. Filing too soon, when you are still speculating as to how the invention works and what its technical advantages are, means you will not have enough meat in your application. Also the clock will start ticking on deadlines for extending your filing to other countries, and those deadlines will arrive all too soon – before you can justify the expense of an international patenting programme.

BRITISH AND IRISH PATENTS: VIA THE NATIONAL ROUTE

Where to File First

You can file an initial patent application in your home country. British subjects, whether UK residents or not, must file at the British or European Patent Office first, or obtain clearance from the British Patent Office to file first in another country. Irish citizens do not have to file in the first instance at the Irish Patents Office.

British Patents

A British patent is granted for a period of twenty years and covers the UK, including Northern Ireland, some present and former British colonies, and most notably can still be extended to cover the Hong Kong Special Administrative Region, by a registration process. It undergoes a full process of search and examination as to novelty and obviousness in the British Patent Office, located in Cardiff.

Accelerated search and examination may be requested and a granted British patent may be obtained in about twelve months, if the right steps are taken. Annual renewal fees are paid from year five onwards to maintain a British patent in force.

Irish Patents

Two types of Irish patent exist: a full-term or 20-year patent, and a short-term or 10-year patent. The Irish Patents Office, located in Kilkenny, does not provide any independent examination.

For a 20-year patent, however, the applicant must provide evidence that his invention is patentable. This usually takes the form of an already granted or European patent, or an official search, which at the moment is actually a search contracted out to the British Patent Office. This is little used, and most 20-year Irish patents granted since 1992 are now granted by the European Patent Office.

The Irish 10-year patent is similar to what is sometimes called a 'petty patent' or 'utility model' in other countries. This is a rubber stamp, registration process, where the Irish Patents Office will grant a 10-year patent, with no search and examination, in about three or four months.

A supposedly lower standard of inventiveness is required, and if you try to enforce an Irish 10-year patent, you have first to show the evidence of patentability that you would for a 20-year patent, but then the amount of money in damages that can be recovered in an infringement action is presently limited to only IR£30,000. Although the system of quick grant may have some virtues, many Irish 10-year patents have probably been granted which are of dubious validity and are of little real value.

EUROPEAN PATENTS

The European Patent Office

The European Patent Office (EPO), located in Munich, was established in 1978, and now covers all of the fifteen EU countries plus Switzerland, Liechtenstein, Monaco and Cyprus, Member States of the European Patent Organisation. It is not an institution of the EU, but is a self-financing organisation established and administered jointly by the national Patent Offices of the Member States to grant patents in a more streamlined and efficient manner.

These goals have certainly been achieved. A single search is now possible that avoids the expensive duplication of effort by the national Patent Offices in the past, and a single examination is possible in English, French or German, the three official EPO languages. The numbers of applications filed have increased steadily (100,000 filed in 1997), which is way in excess of the numbers still handled by the national Patent Offices.

A European Patent is not an EU Patent

However, the goal of a single Community patent covering all EU countries has not yet been realised. When the EPO grants a European patent, it has to be brought into force as separate national patents and registered with each of the national Patent Offices in question, to which an annual renewal fee must be paid.

All non-English speaking countries (except Luxembourg and Monaco) require a translation of the granted European patent specification in their own language, making up maybe half the total cost of obtaining a European patent. Despite this drawback, the cost per country is still much less than the old system of filing separate national patent applications. You do not have to cover all nineteen countries or even all the EU countries, you choose which ones you wish to cover.

The quality of the search and examination is regarded as being one of the best, and a granted European patent ought to be taken very seriously. It is worth the money. Once granted, a European patent can be opposed or challenged by third parties for a period of nine months. About 6 per cent of European patents are opposed, and if overturned, you lose your patent for all your chosen countries.

INTERNATIONAL PATENT APPLICATIONS (PCT)

You cannot get a 'World Patent'

There is no such thing as an international patent or 'world patent' and you ought to be very sceptical about the message 'world patents pending'. Patenting at an international level is extremely expensive. However, about 100 countries have now signed up to the Patent Co-operation Treaty (PCT) which provides for an international patent search and a system of international preliminary examination to be carried out to a unified standard and administered by the World Intellectual Property Office (WIPO) an arm of the United Nations in Geneva.

International Search

You can file an international or PCT application in English at the British, Irish or European Patent Offices. One of its advantages is that it can be filed at the 12-month deadline under the International Patent Convention, for filing in other countries, but effectively keeping open your options as to eventual coverage in most other countries for a further period of time. In other words, you can buy more time.

That period is twenty months from the first or home country application if all you want is the international search, or 30 months if you also want the international preliminary examination. In the long run, this intermediate international route to obtaining national patents will cost you more, but in the shorter term it has the advantage of putting off the decision about patent coverage in expensive countries, such as Japan and the European Patent Office.

International Examination

The International Preliminary Examination gives you a non-binding opinion regarding patentability, in other words a pretty good idea if the national Patent Offices are going to grant a patent or not. If the signs look bad, or if the product is not selling well, you may decide to let the whole thing lapse, before spending any money on national patent applications.

National Phase

The PCT system has been very successful and has done much to relieve the burden of maintaining search documentation and the duplication of effort of examination of applications in Patent Offices around the world. However, on account of the differences in patent laws in different countries, many Patent Offices still want to do their own 'top-up' searches and examination when deciding whether to grant a patent in the so-called 'national phase' of the application.

This is the expensive part, where you are required to have a translation made of your patent specification for proceeding in non-English speaking countries. If you opt for this international route, remember it has an 'international phase', where a single official search and optional examination are carried out by a designated Patent Office, e.g. the British or European Patent Office, and a 'national phase', where your international patent application splits into a series of parallel national patent applications, all dealt with separately by the various national Patent Offices and resulting in a bundle of separate national patents. If you go the international route, it could take you about two years longer to get patents granted in most countries.

Is the International Route for you?

If at the end of the twelve months from your initial patent application, you are certain where your main competition and major markets are located, and your own product is on the market, you are already in a position to decide what other countries should be included in a patenting programme.

You do not have to buy time to decide what to do. You should go straight ahead with say a US and a

European patent application. The international route is not for you and could waste you a lot of money and time. A lot of companies use the PCT system because it puts off making a decision. However in some cases, a decision is difficult to make.

What Countries should you Cover?

The sensible course is not to overstretch your budget and place your patents strategically in the countries where competing *manufacturers* are known or likely to be located, not necessarily the same as your main *market*. If you ever want to enforce your patents to stop infringers, you will want to stop the infringement at source, i.e. the manufacturers, not the customers.

US PATENTS

A Huge Market Covered by a Single Patent

A US patent still represents the best value for money by any standards: a single patent, covering a market of 280 million people. For small companies, qualifying as 'small entities', there is a reduced fee structure, and once granted, unlike other countries with an annual renewal fee, a US patent has only to be renewed four times throughout its 20-year term.

The US Patent System is Different: *'first to invent'*

The patent system in the USA is different to everywhere else. The first person to come up with a particular invention is entitled to *the* patent for that invention. Almost everywhere else, it does not matter who can prove he invented something first, the person entitled to the patent will be the one who files his patent application first at the Patent Office.

The US system is known as 'the first to invent',

and maybe it is fairer, but the 'first to file' system is much simpler. The elaborate system of sorting out disputes between inventors of the same invention is not really used that often. However, any company serious about patenting in the USA must be aware of this and is well advised to keep good, dated written records and logs of their in-house R&D activity. Such records may be crucial in proving when an invention was conceived.

Filing a US Patent Application

A US patent application must be filed at the US Patent and Trademark Office, located in Washington DC, and it has to be filed in the names of the inventors, then later assigned to the company. In any patent application, you have to name the inventors, and you may require a written assignment of rights to the company for the patent to be in the company's name. In the USA it is particularly important to decide who are the inventors are and it is important to get this right from the beginning.

US Patents are Respected

Even if you have no present plans to enter the US market, if you have a US patent you could license out manufacture of the patented product to a US company and earn royalty income. The sheer scale of the market is such that a single licensee can provide a very respectable income stream.

US companies respect patents because they know that they can be put out of business if they do not. Anyone who knowingly infringes a US patent is liable to three times the normal amount of compensatory damages. A case in point is when Kodak infringed a Polaroid patent on instant colour film, in the end having to pay US$873 million in damages.

THE ART OF SEARCHING AND FINDING OTHER PEOPLE'S PATENTS

Several million British patents have been granted. Worldwide, many tens of millions of patent documents exist. The great majority of these have, of course, expired, but they have been published by Patent Offices around the world. The patent system requires this publication; it is part of the bargain. You get a State-sponsored monopoly for a limited time; the State publishes your invention for the benefit of all, who are free to use your invention, which you might otherwise have kept secret, after your patent monopoly expires.

The millions of patents already published are vast repositories of technical information. Recently published patents give you information about the current 'state of the art' in all technical fields and information about what new products your competitors may be just about to put on the market. The older patents give you information about the closest 'prior art', documents pre-dating your own patent application or invention, documents which, no matter how old they are, may still be an obstacle to your patent being granted.

Many people are totally unaware of this sea of information, and how useful it is, whether from a purely technical, marketing or legal standpoint. Here are eight ways this information can be used.

EIGHT WAYS TO USE PATENT INFORMATION

1. **State of the art and technical information for R&D purposes.**

2. **Novelty search:** is your 'invention' new?

3. **Infringement clearance:** do you infringe someone else's patent?

4. **Validity:** will the patent you infringe stand up?

5. **Watching:** trade the progress of a competitor's patent application.

6. **Current awareness**: a weekly search of new patent applications in your field.

7. **Subsequent art:** is your patent being cited against other patents pending?

8. **Retrieve patent documents.**

State of the Art and Technical Information

You are about to embark on a new avenue of research and development. But are you reinventing the wheel? Find out the different ways others may have already approached the same problem, in the last five years, e.g. a particular company in a particular country. The databases make any enquiry possible. Train your R&D people to use them.

Novelty

You are about to file a patent application, but is your invention really new? With a novelty search you attempt to cover as much as you can, as cost effectively as you can. You try to find 'prior art', which might stand in your way, which the Patent Office might find when it does its official search, but you won't have access to the same databases as it has. It may be an inconclusive search and you hope nothing relevant does turn up. Ask your patent attorney to do the search, and specify a budget, e.g. about IR£500.

Infringement Clearance

You are about to put a new product on the home or a foreign market. You have had problems before from a competitor asserting its patents; you do not want problems again. An infringement clearance search is a search confined to all patents in force, relevant to your product, in the country concerned. You want a fairly conclusive result; a lot of money could be at stake. This must be performed by a professional searcher or patent attorney and will cost IR£1,000 or more.

Validity

You have become aware of a competitor's granted patent, which will seriously affect your business, you have been threatened with patent infringement litigation, or you are considering paying quite a lot of money for a licence under a third-party's patent, but is it worth it, is it a strong or a weak patent?

You need to test the strength or validity of someone else's patent to see could it be knocked out (found invalid by a court). A validity search is a rigorous search of the whole published patent literature, best left to professional searchers. It will cost at least IR£5,000 and maybe more, and it will take some months to complete properly and assess the result.

Watching

You find out about a competitor's patent application before it is granted. It may or may not pose a problem to you. You may wish to block the grant or mount a challenge by filing an opposition to grant. A watching search may be set up to monitor the progress of the application through the search and examination stages in the Patent Office and warn you of the date of grant. Your patent attorney can advise you on the steps to take.

Current Awareness

You want to find out who is applying for patents in a narrow subject area of interest to your company, what your competitors are patenting, what new competitors are entering your field. The patent database hosts provide a service where every week, when the just published patent applications are added to the database, your search strategy is run automatically at an off-peak time and the result is mailed to you. This is an excellent and cheap way of keeping abreast of technical developments and competitor activity in your selected subject area. You find out fast and you find out first.

Subsequent Art

You have a granted patent for a successful product. That will stand as 'prior art' against anyone who files a patent, application subsequently for a similar or closely related invention. It may be so close to your patent that a Patent Office will cite your patent in its official search. A subsequent art search will flag this when it happens. It may be an innocent re-inventor of your wheel, or an imitator, a potential infringer or a competitor deliberately trying to 'get around' your patent. In many cases you have nothing to worry about, but at least you find out. This type of search can only be done with the big patent databases.

Document Search

You have details of a patent number from a competitor's literature or marked on its product, e.g. European Patent No. 0,234,567. You would like to see a copy of his granted patent to see what it actually covers or what technical information there is about its composition. You can now download a copy of many patent documents from the internet, free. (See the 'Further Resources' section at the end of this book.)

PITFALLS OF PATENT SEARCHING

- **Keyword search in abstracts: can be very hit and miss.** Full text searching is not yet widely available. The big patent databases such as Derwent's World Patent Index, only have specially written abstracts of patents.

- **Manual searches: best for infringement clearance and validity searches.** Old-fashioned manual searches of paper records are still advised for infringement clearance and validity searches, therefore these are expensive. For these types of searches, no stone should be left unturned.

- **You cannot search unpublished material.** US patents are not published until they are granted. There can therefore be a time lag of about three years or more before you find out about a competitor's US patent. Other countries publish patent applications within eighteen months of the basic application in the home country. Competitor activity may therefore have been kept secret for up to eighteen months previous to your search.

BLUFF AND DETERRENT VALUE OF 'PATENTS PENDING'

The Patent Portfolio

Playing the patent game can be a bit like poker. Bluff can be as important as having a good hand. Many big companies have a patent department and an in-house patent attorney. Their job is to identify patent opportunities and build a patent portfolio.

With this sort of operation, you can be sure that not every one of the patents will be particularly strong, or may be for some quite small improvement in a product or process. But taken together, they form a wall around the company's intellectual property. If one brick falls, there are others.

Big companies have big patent portfolios – but it could be a big bluff. Sometimes a strong 'basic patent' for a particular invention cannot be obtained because of a disclosure or the company simply did not realise what a good idea it had until after the product hit the market (too late to apply for a patent then). All that is left is to patent the process by which it is made, and different and later improvements or versions of the same product. These are weak patents. The company hopes they will be infringed by someone copying the basic invention.

The portfolio idea is also used defensively. Big companies build up large numbers of patents to use as wild cards in the poker game. Bargaining counters to get you out of trouble. A's patents block B; B's patents block A. The two can pool their patents, and agree not to sue, on a royalty-free basis, or for an agreed sum transferred from the one with the least bargaining counters or the weakest patents. If one had no wild cards, he could be out of the game, quite literally.

Very Big Portfolios Make a Very Big Wall

Some big US companies play the game very aggressively and will relentlessly pursue smaller fry for licence fees knowing their patents are unlikely to be challenged, because of their corporate might and/or the sheer weight of their patent portfolio.

A Small Wall can be just as Good

Smaller companies can learn some lessons from the way the big boys play the game. If you believe you have a real breakthrough invention, get your patent attorney's advice as to every conceivable way of patenting it. A small wall of five or six patents could make it very hard for anyone to find a way around your invention. If it is very successful, you will be copied; attempts to copy are really the accolade if all truly successful inventions. You will want to ward off such attempts.

Patent Pending and Deterrent Value

If your invention is not a great technical break-through, but nevertheless likely to be a successful product on the market, what do you do? Apply to patent it anyway.

The improvement may be very small, your patent application may only scrape through, but from the day you apply, you can put 'patent pending' on literature and packaging. This has a deterrent value in itself. You have to wait until your patent has been granted before you could enforce your rights against an imitator or infringer, but compensatory damages can be claimed back to an earlier date under a system of 'provisional protection'. Someone who copies you during the 'patent pending' period before grant does so at their peril.

Patent Pending and Bluff

Also remember that your patent application will not be published by the Patent Office for about eighteen months – this means that it will be impossible for anyone else to see its contents: and how strong or how weak the patent is likely to be cannot really be determined properly.

During that period, you are playing a blinder,

and you are not compelled to show your hand. What better bluff? When granted, a weak patent will be vulnerable to attack, but if it is indeed a very successful product on the market, that very fact will help you to defend your patent. Commercial success, and copying by competitors, are both arguments against the contention that your patent covers no more than obvious improvements. (See Chapter 9).

REMEMBER

DO:

- Realise that it can take several years to obtain a granted patent, but the process can be put on a 'fast track' if you ask.

- Know that most patents are granted for small improvements, a really ground-breaking innovation is not required.

- Engage a patent attorney.

- Consider carefully the different routes available for obtaining patents internationally and which is the most cost effective.

- Recognise that there are strong patents and weak patents and know how to play the game of bluff.

DO NOT:

- Spend money on a patent application unless your patent attorney has first carried out some searches or can give you some indication that a patent will be granted – you will not get a refund.

- Presume that it is difficult to get a patent, but any document pre-dating your application which describes the same invention or something very similar will prevent you getting a patent.

- Try to file a patent application and deal directly with the Patent Office yourself.

- Forget to ask your patent attorney how much the whole process will cost, from application to grant, and then the cost of renewing your patent.

- Underestimate the bluff and deterrent value of 'patent pending', even if you have a relatively weak patent application.

Chapter 6

Choosing And Protecting A Brand Name: A Trade Mark Strategy For Your Company

This chapter will help you to:

- understand what the essence of a brand is;
- realise what a vital role trade mark registration plays in protecting your brands.

Choosing And Protecting A Brand Name: A Trade Mark Strategy For Your Company

The most important assets are brands. Buildings age and become dilapidated. Machines wear out. Cars rust. People die. But what lives on are brands.

> Former chairman, United Biscuits Ltd, maker of 'McVities'

WHAT IS A TRADE MARK?

A trade mark is a name, sign or symbol used to distinguish the products, or services, of one business enterprise from those of others. The maximum legal protection can only be secured by registration. The best thing about a registered trade mark is that it can be maintained in force indefinitely, unlike a patent, which has a limited term of twenty years.

The cost of maintenance is also significantly less; whereas a patent has to be renewed by paying an annual renewal fee, a registered trade mark has only to be renewed once every ten years. There was a time, quite recently, when a trade mark could only be registered for goods, but now services are included, sometimes known as a service mark, when used exclusively to denote a service.

EXAMPLES OF TRADE MARKS

Type of Trade Mark	Example
Invented words	Kodak, Pepsi, Lego, Pentium

Ordinary words	Visa, Penguin, Mars
Letters	AT&T, IBM, BP, HB
A logo style	Coca-Cola's copper-plate logo
Numbers	4711, 555, No.5, 99
Numbers and words	7-Up, Windows 98
Symbols	the Bass red triangle, Coca-Cola ribbon device, Dulux English sheep dog, Lacoste crocodile
Labels	on wine bottles
Surnames	McDonald's, Guinness, Colman's, Benson & Hedges
Place names	Waterford, Ballygowan, Halifax
Signatures	those of (Henry) Ford, Johnny Walker, (Arthur) Guinness
Shapes	Coca-Cola bottle, Toblerone chocolate bar
Sounds	musical jingles, MGM Lion's roar, sound of sheepdog barking (Dulux)
Smells	dewberry (Body Shop)

Colours	Kodak (yellow), BP (green)
Slogans	'I Can't Believe It's Not Butter' (a non-butter dairy spread), 'Don't Leave Home Without It' (American Express), 'It's The Real Thing' (Coca-Cola)

WHAT IS A BRAND?

A brand may involve many related trade marks, as can be seen from the *Coca-Cola* examples given above. The above examples are nearly all registered trade marks. The individual elements of a brand could be registered separately (the best option) or in combination (not good, but sometimes necessary).

Brands Evolve

A brand evolves in time and subtle changes, in the logo used, the shade of colour and design features, may have to be made from time to time, to modernise the brand image, to give it a facelift. Consistency is very important in a brand, and the underlying function of the brand – to clearly distinguish your goods and services from others – must never be forgotten. You do not often see radical changes in brands – like *Pepsi* going blue, but subtle changes are made all the time; Shell's yellow scallop shell logo is quite different now from what it was twenty years ago. Each time these changes are made, the new trade mark has to be registered again to obtain full protection.

A Relentless Battle to Protect a Big Brand

We often associate single colours with brands (e.g.

red for *Coca-Cola*), but they can be very difficult to monopolise. One thing in common with all the big brands, which are known globally, is the absolute rock on which they have been built – intellectual property protection. The big brand companies spend a lot of money and effort in ensuring that their trade marks are registered in all markets, that those registrations are properly maintained and managed, that infringers and look-alikes are dealt with swiftly by actually enforcing their trade mark rights. It is a relentless battle.

> **WORD TO THE WISE**
> A brand will only remain powerful if its owners take very great care to protect it.

The reason why, to this day, a soft drink from extracts of kola nut invented by a pharmacist over a 100 years ago, which he called *Coca-Cola*, so dominates the soft drinks industry, bears testimony to that. Following the early success of this product, literally hundreds of the early competing products were beaten off. Only one (*Pepsi*) remains a serious contender. *Coca-Cola* is also fairly unique in being equally well known by two trade marks, *Coca-Cola* and *Coke*, apparently the two most universally understood words by the non-English speaking world.

BRAND POWER

A brand is only a powerful brand if its owners take very great care to protect it. Competitors will dream up every conceivable way to cash in on the brand owner's reputation and the goodwill of its customers and, if they are allowed to get away with it, they will. That will steadily injure and devalue the brand.

The purpose and function of a trade mark is quite simply to provide the means by which those customers, many of them very loyal customers, associate a product with you. But around that product you have built a reputation for quality, consistency, by your advertising and promotion you have built an 'image' to appeal to your customers, which in itself is of tremendous importance and which takes time to develop. This, the magical 'goodwill' factor, also called 'brand equity'. This is what a powerful brand also conveys.

Never Abandon a Trade Mark and its Goodwill

If you have been using a particular trade mark for a relatively long time, you should never let it go. Change it slightly; let it evolve, but never abandon it. For if you do, you abandon that intangible goodwill, and it may quickly be forgotten.

Again, let's look at what *Coca-Cola* did. In countries where less and less of their sales were in the famous waisted and fluted bottle, the value of the bottle as a trade mark was in decline. Just in time, they registered a *picture* of the *Coca-Cola* bottle as a trade mark and that now appears as a separate trade mark on their cans. In countries where it has been possible to do so, the actual *shape* of the bottle has been registered as a separate trade mark.

What Makes a Powerful Brand?

Powerful brands have to be *instantly* recognisable. This is often achieved by limiting the choice of colours used and by incorporating a strong symbol or logo as integral elements of the brand. Look back at the list of things that can make a trade mark – *words* are only one of them. If your branded product is destined for export markets in non-English speaking countries, will your chosen brand name travel and will it be as easily recognised and pronounced?

Does it have any meaning or connotation in other languages and cultures? You will not see *Persil* on sale in France, because that it the French word for parsley and that somehow does not work as a brand name for soap powder. *Kodak* is an entirely invented word, apparently without meaning in any well-known language and is easy to pronounce. The yellow packaging and red stripe logo have added greatly to the power of the *Kodak* brand.

Some Brands don't Travel

Here are some examples of brands, which may work well on natives in their own markets, but would definitely not travel to our English-speaking world.

Kräpp	a German brand of toilet paper
Bimbo	a French brand of bread
Nora Knackers	a Scandinavian brand of crispbread crackers.

SLOGANS

Watch out for slogans, which work well in one culture but when translated into other languages may not do so well. *Kentucky Fried Chicken's* 'Finger Lickin' Good' slogan was a disaster in Japanese, because in Japan, it is just not the done thing to lick your fingers when eating.

One has to be especially careful with slogans. They must be short and snappy, convey your message and say something about your company's mission – all quite hard to do in a few words. They can be overdone as advertising slogans and can therefore grow stale. American companies seem to know how to get the best out of slogans. They just appear as subtitles, and they change; e.g. *Delta Airlines* 'We love to fly and it shows'; 'You'll love the way we fly'; 'On top of the world'. Slogans add image to a brand, and a 'feel good' factor to already loyal customers.

SYMBOLS AND LOGOS

The most powerful brands are those which are reduced down to an instantly recognisable symbol, often cherished for its pure simplicity. The *Bass* beer red triangle, the *Nike* 'tick', the three stripes of *Adidas*, the *McDonald's* golden arch 'M'. Consider that any child, old enough to utter its first words, will gleefully shout from its child seat in the back of the car *McDonald's*, on passing the last of those. That is brand power. In fact, a surprising proportion of your market, including children, may actually be illiterate and symbols are the only element of the brand they can recognise!

There is no doubt that logos are the most powerful element in a brand, but the beauty of the best ones is in their simplicity. However, brands have to be distinctive – too simple means too commonplace and therefore not distinctive at all. It takes a long time and a lot of advertising budget to make a triangle, a tick, three stripes or the letter 'M' truly distinctive symbols. For the small to medium-sized company something with more design elements, maybe capable of being simplified in time, would be better.

INVENTED WORDS

From the point of view of obtaining a registered trade mark, invented words make the best trade marks. They are absolutely distinctive, can have little or no reference to the goods or services which they denote and are easy to register for that reason. You have to use imagination. *Simplex* is no good – it has been registered for practically every type of goods already. All drugs are branded with invented words e.g. *Viagra, Tagamet, Panadol,* etc. Invented words are not quite so easy to remember, but their inherent distinctive character makes them have potential as great brands: easy to protect, easy to defend and easy to come up with one that does not have the wrong connotation in a foreign language, i.e. in export markets.

ORDINARY WORDS

Ordinary words make very good trade marks and are a bit easier to remember than a purely invented word. However, they must have a distinctive character and not have any direct association with the goods or services or the way in which the goods are used. If they do, they may be rejected as registered trade marks as being devoid of distinctive character.

When choosing a new brand name, this is the most common trap to fall into. But surely a good brand *describes* in some way my goods or services? For example, *Kwik-Fit* (quick fit) for a car repair service, *Lyk-Nu* (like new) for a dry cleaners, do not become any more distinctive by spelling them phonetically. They tell you, in a pretty direct way, what will or should happen when you use the service.

Ordinary words, when chosen as a brand name, should really have absolutely no reference or association with the product itself. *Coke* does not make you think of a type of coal, nor *Mars* a planet, when you are in a sweet shop.

However, you can be clever in choosing an ordinary word, which although not having any real connection or direct association, does have some sideways or indirect association. You might be inclined think of your *Visa* card as your 'passport' to spending money, anywhere. These words with 'covert allusion' can be registered quite easily and are very clever trade marks.

PLACE NAMES AND PROPER NAMES

Since a registered trade mark gives you a virtual monopoly (an exclusive legal right) to use a particular name in relation to a particular product or service, you are not allowed in law to monopolise names which anybody, or certain people, can legitimately use. Place names are an example.

In theory, anyone should be entitled to make glass in Waterford and call it Waterford Glass. In practice, one company had to do so for a very long time, and earn a very substantial reputation by so doing, before exclusive rights to *Waterford* as a registered trade mark became possible. The larger the place, the longer you may have to wait, before you can eventually succeed in getting the full protection which registration gives you. Even small places, unknown to anyone outside your country, or part of your country, will not be capable of registration. Not straight away.

Worse still are proper names, people's names. If you try to register a trade mark, which is a person's surname or sounds very like one, it will be rejected, unless it is a very rare surname. Of course there are examples of surnames which are registered trade marks, such as *Guinness*, *McDonald's*, *Ford*, etc. but again they have had to earn their exclusivity by long usage.

If your name happened to be *Johnny Walker* or *Jack Daniels*, you could not be prevented from selling whiskey using your own name as your trade mark. Of course you would be quite lucky if one of those were your name and you had a legitimate liquor business, because you would no doubt be a thorn in someone else's side – and you might be bought out! A place exists in the Czech Republic called Budweis where beer is brewed by the 'Budweiser' method, and this was a thorn to Anheuser Busch Inc., makers of *Budweiser*, as it was a legitimate use of a little known place name.

You have to hand it to *Häagen-Dazs*, a brand of ice cream. It sounds like a surname, or maybe a place name, but it is not; it was made up. Deliberately exotic, exclusive or whatever – but whatever it is, it has been a very successful brand!

COMPANY NAMES

The registration of a company's name in the Companies Office as a company or business name gives no exclusive rights to that name. Generally it means that another company with exactly the same name cannot trade under that name. But one can with a very similar name. Company names can also become registered trade marks, which means that exclusive rights are obtained, extending to similar sounding and confusingly similar names. Abbreviated names, such as *IBM* (International Business Machines), *AT&T* (American Telephone & Telegraph) and *BP* (British Petroleum), can eventually become registered trade marks.

Abbreviations can be turned into words, such as *ESSO* (SO for Standard Oil). A company really should even consider changing its name so that the name can itself be registered as a trade mark. This will give the wonderful possibilities of making the company's name, its whole image in fact, into a brand. One that can be protected indefinitely with the full exclusive rights that trade mark registration gives. This could be done by abbreviating the existing company name, taking some familiar element of it or by creating a new logo.

NUMBERS

Numbers do not make good trade marks and are difficult to register. They are not really very distinctive, and why should anyone be allowed to monopolise some numbers, which might be used as part numbers of batch numbers in any case? *Windows 98, VAT*

69, Boeing 747, Mazda 323, for example may have been registered, but exclusive rights will not be given for the numbers which form an element of those trade marks. Trade marks which consist of numbers and nothing else are really quite rare, *4711,* an eau-de cologne, being one well-known example.

SIGNATURES

Everyone's signature is different, so signatures are absolutely distinctive. But they do not make very good trade marks. It is hard to think of any that are so famous that they would be instantly recognisable, or even legible. Distinctiveness

> **WORD TO THE WISE**
> Distinctiveness is no good if the trade mark is not recognisable and easy to remember.

is no good if the trade mark is not recognisable and easy to remember. The signature of a company's founder, for example, is a good element of a brand, denoting a seal of quality and the company's longevity. Signatures can be stylised like that of the trade marks, *Ford,* (Henry Ford, founder of Ford Motors), *Walt Disney,* in an easily legible form.

SHAPES, SOUNDS AND SMELLS

With recent changes in trade mark legislation in Ireland, the UK and the EU, virtually anything which is not 'devoid of distinctive character' can now be registered as a trade mark. The actual shape of a product, or its container or packaging, can, in time, become a potent brand symbol. The triangular shape of the *Toblerone* chocolate bar, the *Coca-Cola* bottle, are really trade marks in themselves.

Distinctive containers are normally protected first of all by design registration (see Chapter 7) but design registrations eventually expire. If a shape becomes so distinctive of your product after that amount of time, there is no doubt that it could then be registered as a trade mark and so given indefinite protection. This possibility of an indefinite monopoly is what is so valuable about trade mark registration.

SOUNDS

Sounds as registered trade marks are a new idea and not many have been registered so far. One cannot think that by some Pavlovian response, one will buy *Dulux* paint when hearing an English sheep dog bark, but its bark has been registered as a trade mark, in addition of course, to its image. It is worth mentioning here that if you have a word trade mark which has been registered, someone will infringe your rights *speaking* your trade mark, for example in a radio advertisement.

SMELLS

You may think it bizarre, but smells can be very distinctive of a product and can have either a strong or even subliminal association with your goods or services. The perfume industry spends a huge amount of time and money to develop a new scent, and then to brand and market it. It can have a long product life and the scent itself, and not just the brand name, can become sufficiently distinctive to be a trade mark in its own right. The brand is often extended from the designer label fashion business.

A smell may now be registered as a trade mark if the active scent constituents can be represented by a chemical formula, which is how it must actually be registered at the Trade Mark Registry. Another example, a subliminal association really, is the dewberry scent that wafts out the door of every *Body Shop*. A blind person would know he was in that particular retail outlet, and the smell is deliberately generated, it is not an accident. That is a trade mark and it could be registered.

COLOURS

Colours can, with difficulty, be registered as trade marks. On their own, unless used consistently in relation to the brand, in an almost wall to wall fashion, a single colour is unlikely to have the power and potential to distinguish your product from everyone else's. *BP* decided to use its green from its yellow and green logo in advertising, forecourts, etc. and eventually to register the colour as a trade mark. The deep yellow used by *Kodak* on *all* its products is identified as a trade mark, but you need a pretty big market share for your product before colour begins to become a distinctive factor in your brand.

Single colours are inherently not that distinctive, but combinations can become so. Some colours may have become non-distinctive. Supermarket shelves display branded products and non-branded or 'own brand' products beside each other in similar coloured containers, e.g. blue for bleach, etc. The colour, or colour combination, has to be actually *capable* of distinguishing the goods. This is not so easy in practice. However, consistency, and the wall to wall coverage approach used by *BP* and *Kodak* show how even a single colour can become one of the most potent brand symbols of all.

HOW ARE TRADE MARKS REGISTERED?

Clearance Searches are Vital

You should employ a trade mark agent (see Chapter 4) who will handle these searches and advise generally on the best scope of protection, which you can obtain. Once you have decided on a shortlist of new potential trade marks, your trade mark agent will advise which are capable of being registered and will carry out searches to determine whether or not any of these is too close or confusingly similar with an existing registered trade mark.

These clearance searches are vitally important. If the Trade Mark Registry (a part of the Patent Office) finds that it has already registered a closely similar mark for the same or similar goods, your application for registration will be refused. If it is redundant or not 'in use', you might possibly be able to have the conflicting registration removed. If the other party is not using the previously registered trade mark on all the goods and services listed in his registration, the overlap might hopefully not matter; it might be possible to negotiate a consent from the other party for your registration to co-exist with theirs, subject to the Trade Mark Registry's agreement. These are messy situations, and it would have been better to choose a mark in the first place which you are clear to register and free to use, from day one.

Make sure Registration is as Wide in Scope as Possible

Consider very carefully the list of goods and services for which registration is sought. The trade mark can be registered based upon a clear *intention* to use the mark on *all* the goods and services specified, so you have to advise your trade mark agent on your present and *future* marketing plans for that brand. If you have a word mark, used in a particularly distinctive logotype (script or font) it should be registered twice. Once in 'block capitals', which means all logotypes are covered; secondly in the actual logotype as used. Your trade mark agent should advise you on what actual steps must be taken to secure the widest scope of protection by registration and it may involve multiple trade mark applications.

SINGLE EUROPEAN COMMUNITY TRADE MARK

It is now possible to make a single trade mark application to the Community Trade Marks Office, an EU institution, located in Alicante, Spain. This has considerable advantages, but some disadvantages:

ADVANTAGES OF
A COMMUNITY TRADE MARK (CTM)

- A single registration for all EU countries.

- Do not have to use CTM in every EU country to maintain registration.

- Cost, compared to fifteen national registrations, is much less.

- A single legal action to restrain infringement in the whole of the EU.

- CTM application can be converted to national applications.

DISADVANTAGES OF
A COMMUNITY TRADE MARK (CTM)

- CTM application/registration can be opposed /invalidated if prior conflicting right in *any* EU country.

- Losing party in opposition bears all costs. Oppositions are quite common.

REMEMBER

DO:

- Apply to register your trade marks – only registration can give you strong legal rights.

- Choose distinctive, non-descriptive trade marks as these are the easiest to register.

- Be aware that a brand evolves, subtle changes may be made to your trade mark – it may have to be registered again.

- Know that a registered trade mark specifies listed goods and/or services – use it with new goods and services and you may not be covered.

- Employ a trade mark agent to handle all trade mark registrations and advise you.

DO NOT:

- Launch a new brand before your trade mark agent has carried out trade mark clearance searches.

- Choose non-distinctive words which describe the product, they are difficult to register and make poor trade marks.

- Choose non-distinctive surnames and geographical names as trade marks, they are very difficult to register.

- Abandon a trade mark, as with it you abandon intangible goodwill and brand equity.

- Be complacent; it requires very great care and relentless effort to protect a powerful brand.

Chapter 7

The Importance Of Copyright And Design Protection

This chapter will help you to:

- understand the principles of how copyright works;

- understand how copyright differs from patents, its strengths and weaknesses compared with patents;

- understand in more detail how industrial designs are protected by design registration.

The Importance Of Copyright And Design Protection

> Art has to move you and design does not, unless it's a good design for a bus.
>
> David Hockney

COPYRIGHT

Of all the branches of intellectual property law, copyright is probably the most misunderstood. Yet we are all exposed to the very existence of copyright on an almost daily basis: the copyright notices that you click past on your computer, the ubiquitous copyright symbol ©, acknowledgements of copyright in small print in newspapers, books, tapes, CDs, photographs, videos, movies, even on your company's own product literature and packaging.

Copyright certainly applies to a vast array of different things. All of these are copyright 'works'.

WHAT ARE COPYRIGHT WORKS?

- They involve the creation and expression of an 'artistic' or 'literary' work.

- There was an originator or author.

- The work was original, independently created and not copied from someone else.

AN ARTISTIC OR LITERARY WORK

A copyright 'work' can be practically anything that the human intellect is capable of creating directly or indirectly; for an artistic work, there is no test for artistic merit. Such a test would anyway be quite impossible to frame in law, since artistic appeal, like beauty, is certainly in the eye of the beholder. A literary work likewise qualifies for copyright protection irrespective of true literary qualities.

The important thing is that the ideas are *expressed* in a tangible form and recorded, whether on paper, film, magnetic tape or whatever. A copyright work does not even have to be legible or make any sense. A simple sketch on the back of an envelope, or a detailed production drawing are both copyright works. A poem in English or a computer program in a programming language are both copyright works.

'Artistic' works include works of craftsmanship and sculpture, things which are hand-made, one of a kind, but in Ireland copyright does *not* cover three-dimensional designs, in particular those which are mass-produced or industrially produced. In the UK, the latter may be protected by an 'unregistered design right'.

THE AUTHOR

It is very important to identify the author of the copyright work and, of course, this may be more than one person. The legal right of copyright lies first and foremost with the author, who can, and usually must, assign his or her copyright to someone else, e.g. a publisher or an employer. Put a standard clause in employment contracts, or have a standard assignment, where authors (employees, contractors, consultants) assign their copyright to your company.

AN ORIGINAL WORK

'Original' here does not mean the same as 'new', 'novel' or 'never done before'. Copyright will exist as soon as this 'work' is independently created and given a tangible expression by someone – someone who did not copy it from someone else. This is where people get confused between copyright and patents.

THE DIFFERENCE BETWEEN COPYRIGHT AND PATENTS

Copyright is a legal right, which allows the author of a work to prevent others from copying it without his/her permission.

Unlike patents, copyright does not give exclusive or monopoly rights. What this means is that if you created something which was genuinely all your own work, and you then discovered someone else had, equally genuinely, created exactly the same thing, both of you would be entitled to copyright, independently, for the same work.

For example, this could arise in the case of a photograph of a famous building, taken independently by two photographers, with the same angle, same lighting conditions, etc. However, if the two photographers had independently invented a new tripod for their cameras, both of them could not obtain a patent.

Also, if one of them had obtained a patent, he could actually enforce it against the other, because a patent does give you a monopoly right. The other poor fellow might have to stop selling his tripods or pay a royalty to the patent holder, and might not be entitled to say, "but this was my idea". Both of them had the idea for the tripod – only one of them came up with it first, only one could have got to the Patent Office to file a patent application first, and only one could have exploited and shown his idea to the public first.

These factors will decide who is entitled to a patent, and whether it will be valid and enforceable. For a patent to be valid, your idea must not only have been 'original' in the copyright sense, it must also have been 'novel' when you created it, meaning that it was not known to the public, on the day in which your patent application was filed at the Patent Office.

COPYRIGHT DOES NOT PROTECT IDEAS

Copyright does not protect ideas – only the actual expression of those ideas. Patents, on the other hand, are the only real way to protect the general inventive concept behind an idea, what is clever in a technical sense. The photographers, in the example above, could not patent a photograph. They could patent the tripod, the camera, the lens, the film, anything in which they have made a technical advance, which has not been done before.

> **WORD TO THE WISE**
> Copyright does not protect ideas – only the actual expression of those ideas.

Many people believe that copyright gives protection for general ideas, but it does not – it is a very specific and narrow legal right applying to one particular version of a work, and all it really says is that this version of the work cannot be copied or plagiarised. A patent is a much stronger and wider legal right applying to many versions of a generalised concept and covers independent creation by others, even those who say they thought of the idea first, but cannot prove that the public were aware of this.

STRENGTHS OF COPYRIGHT

Copyright is nevertheless a very important legal right and has many strengths.

- **It takes no time to obtain.** You could wait several years for a patent to be granted. Copyright begins from the moment the 'work' is recorded.

- **It is automatic.** There is no registration system for copyright. You do not have to apply to the Patent Office or anywhere else to register or record your rights. A non-mandatory registration system does exist in the USA, which gives stronger copyright in the USA.

- **It is free!** And not many things in life are. No fees to the Patent Office, patent attorneys, lawyers or anyone else.

- **It is easy to know if you are infringing another copyright.** When creating new software, new advertising slogans, point of sale material, new packaging designs, a new internet website, company manuals, address lists, etc. *Do Not Copy From Elsewhere*. It is that simple; if you can prove that it is all your own original material or that you have a copyright licence (i.e. you are in fact authorised to copy from elsewhere), you cannot be guilty of copyright infringement. In contrast, to find out if you might be infringing anyone else's patents will be difficult and will involve fairly costly searches, and professional opinions, to get a definitive answer.

WEAKNESSES OF COPYRIGHT

- **It does not protect ideas**, as such. Only the actual physical expression of the idea is covered. This does extend a little to cover slight changes from the original. Copyright also covers translations and adaptations of the original work. This includes in the case of software, expressions of the same program in a different programming language and covers source code and object or machine code (ones and zeros). An adaptation can be an abstract or summary or magazine article based on a book, or an extract of music. In short, copyright does cover more than mere slavish copying of an original work, but only derivative works and in no way can it ever cover a basic idea or concept expressed in a non-derivative or substantially different way.

- **It is a non-exclusive right.** The non-exclusive nature of copyright can be a drawback but in practice it does not matter that much. However, it should be remembered that the exclusive, monopoly rights given by patents and, as we shall see later in this chapter, by registered designs, are very valuable.

- **Copyright can be easily exploited and abused.** Take something you would like to copy and there will be some way around it. If it is very simple there may not be. The basic ideas can usually be expressed in a different way. The more and more you introduce original thought and design features, the further you get from the thing that gave you the idea.

  Of course, most copyright infringement, which is endemic in many industries, is of the blatant sort. In other words, counterfeiting. Copying itself is very easy and it is very hard to police and protect oneself, even by asserting copyright. With the new global economy, and electronic commerce, it is going to become even harder. It is an unfortunate fact of life that copyright is not respected. On the other hand, patents are more respected, and can be very difficult to 'get around'.

COPYRIGHT	PATENTS
Strengths	**Weaknesses**
• No time to obtain.	• Takes on average two years to obtain.
• Automatic protection.	• Must apply to Patent Office.
• It's free!	• Obtaining patents is expensive.
• Easy to know if you are infringing another copyright.	• Hard and costly to find if you are infringing another patent.
Weaknesses	**Strengths**
• Does not protect idea as such.	• As near as you will get to protecting general idea.
• Non-exclusive right.	• Monopoly right.
• Hard to enforce, copying is so easy and widespread.	• Can be very difficult to get around.
• Relatively easy to get around.	• A strong patent is a formidable weapon, a deterrent.

INTERNATIONAL ASPECTS OF COPYRIGHT

Nearly all countries of the world belong to the Universal Copyright Convention and the Berne Convention. These confer reciprocal rights to authors of copyright works in different countries. If a copyright exists in one country, it can be extended so as to be subject to the copyright laws of another country, belonging to the same

Convention. The Universal Copyright Convention provides for compulsory marking of a work with the format:

© Copyright Holder's Name, Year (of first publication).

This marking should be placed prominently on all copyright material. Moreover, it stands as a warning that you will assert your copyright, and enforce it, if need be.

INTERNET

There is a lot of copyright infringement going on at present on the internet, in the mistaken belief that:
a) it is all for free anyway;
b) it cannot be detected;
c) there is no international law of copyright.

Copyright infringement on the internet can be detected easily and while there is, as yet, no international law of copyright, this will not stop violators being sued in their own country.

TERM OF COPYRIGHT

Copyright lasts for a very long time. This has now been standardised throughout the EU for literary and artistic works as the author's lifetime plus 70 years (in Ireland and the UK the extra period was 50 years). For all practical purposes, you hardly have to worry about the expiry date of copyright.

COPYRIGHT INFRINGEMENT

You have to prove that copying has occurred, which sometimes can be a headache but is generally not very difficult and, in fact, is usually fairly obvious.

The burden of proof may even shift to the defendant, which means that the infringer may have to prove that he has not copied from you. This puts the copyright holder in a much stronger position.

Copyright law is complex as it strives to cover so many different things. In fact the law always seems to lag behind technology and successive changes have widened the definitions to cover computer software and now electronic commerce.

The important thing that distinguishes a copyright infringement action from a patent infringement action is the amount of monetary damages that a court can award against the infringer, in addition that is, to the destruction of the infringing copies.

Up to the total value of the infringing copies can be recovered in damages called 'conversion damages'. Very substantial fines and even a prison sentence can be imposed under new legislation in Ireland, and the trend is to criminalise copyright infringement, which is, after all, theft. The software industry has long campaigned for more fearsome measures to be taken against copyright infringers, which cost the industry millions of pounds in lost revenue. However, soon the illicit use of software by unlicensed users will be very difficult as the industry is busy developing 'electronic licences', controlled by the vendor.

ANTI-COUNTERFEITING MEASURES

Imports of counterfeit goods, and counterfeit branded goods can often be prevented using Customs Regulations without resort to copyright law, and so provide a fairly instant remedy. However, instant action is required, your solicitor has to move quickly. The idea is to cause trouble for the importer or distributor.

THREE-DIMENSIONAL DESIGNS: REGISTERED DESIGN PROTECTION

Copyright covers practically everything which is two-dimensional: the written word, including the code in computer software, drawings, artwork, graphics, photographs, etc., but what about three-dimensional creations: such as industrially-produced moulded articles, even the moulds themselves, containers, tools, utensils, electrical appliances, computer consoles, keyboards, furniture; consumable goods including soap bars, toothbrushes, pharmaceutical tablets, pasta shapes, confectionery, chocolates, fuel briquettes; building materials, including ceramic tiles, bricks, doors, window frames; valuable goods like jewellery, medals, plaques; larger scale designs for car bodies, aeroplanes, even ships hulls. All of those, provided they have even the slightest degree of aesthetic appeal, are capable of design registration.

REGISTERED DESIGNS: HOW TO GET ONE

By a relatively straightforward process of making an application to the Designs Registry (a part of the Patent Office), a new and original design for an industrially produced article can be registered, normally quite quickly, within about six months.

The application consists of line drawings or photographs of the article bearing the design, the production model, in all views (front, rear, side elevation, top and bottom plan views) so that anyone can see from the accompanying Registered Design Certificate, what the design looks like, in three dimensions. The Patent Office will explain how to go about it, or you can employ a patent attorney to handle the application, which is advisable.

REGISTERED DESIGNS: SCOPE OF PROTECTION

A Registered Design is a Monopoly

A registered design confers the same monopoly protection as a patent. This is what is so good about design registration. It means you can use it to stop someone else who produces the same, or a very similar design, for the same article of manufacture, even if the other person did *not* copy your design and came up with his design quite independently. You could not do this with copyright. However, while copyright is automatic registered design protection is not.

How to Apply

You must apply to the Designs Registry, and you must make you application *before* the product bearing the design is put on the market or the design is unveiled to the public. Again this is similar to patent protection, you cannot get a patent if the product has already been sold or shown in public.

Once you have applied for design registration and/or a patent, you are free to sell the product from the same day on which application(s) are filed at the Patent Office. You do not have to wait until the design has actually been registered or the patent granted. The two types of protection can exist in parallel for the same product. The registered design would cover the external shape of the product; a patent might cover its internal workings or the process by which it was made.

What is Covered by Registration?

Small changes made to the actual design, mould alterations, slight variants, would be covered by the design registration, but any significant changes might not be. All variants of a design, and updated designs, will have to be registered separately. In Ireland and the UK only one design can be covered in a single, application, but a single EU design registration system is proposed and will soon be available, where multiple designs can be covered in a single design registration. Small to medium-sized companies should be aware of this development as it will greatly reduce the costs of registering designs in Europe and give strong, uniform protection for the whole EU territory.

Parts of Design and Colours

It is possible to register a design in respect of a *part* of an article, which can be a very useful device. For example, *Lego* has registered an original flower shaped stud on a toy building block; much better than registering the design of every single type of toy building block with this new stud shape.

If colour combinations represent a design feature, those can be registered, but single colours, as such, are generally not taken to be a design feature.

REGISTERED DESIGNS: TERM OF PROTECTION

At present there is very little uniformity in the term of protection, or its scope, and the laws giving protection to designs are hopelessly out of date in most European countries. However, a single design registration system for all Member States of the EU is proposed and will be available in a few years.

In Ireland the term is fifteen years, in the UK 25 years. A renewal fee is paid every five years, not annually as in the case of patents.

REGISTERED DESIGNS: WHAT CANNOT BE PROTECTED

Entirely Functional Designs

Aesthetic quality or 'eye appeal' is essential. Designs, which are *entirely* functional, where every single feature of design is dictated by a functional requirement of the article, cannot be registered. Machines and internal parts of machinery, fittings, brackets, screws, etc. fall into this category. However, if there is a rounded corner here, an embellishment there, any little feature which serves no real or mechanical function, there is room for protection by way of design registration. The degree of aesthetic quality required can be that low.

Immovable Articles

Designs cannot be registered for immovable articles, such as buildings, but could be for transportable prefabricated units.

Abstract Designs

Designs cannot be registered in the abstract; it must be specified what article has this special shape or design. For example, if a company registers a design for a mobile phone, and an exact replica of this is made as a toy or a pencil case; the toy maker would not infringe the registered design, because the same design has not been applied to the same article.

No Definable or Constant Shape

There can be objections to the registration of a design in which the shape varies in use. This applies to clothing where the shape of the wearer varies, quite considerably! In any case since clothing designs are changed so frequently as fashions change, the clothing industry makes very little use of the design registration system.

This last point is worth remembering. There is little point in registering designs at all if they will be changed in a short time.

TWO-DIMENSIONAL DESIGNS

A registered design may be obtained for a two-dimensional graphic design as applied to some industrially produced article, such as textile, fabric, wallpaper and carpet. Generally, the subject would be a repeating design unit. It could be a printed article, such as a lottery card or ticket, or it could be a design transferred or printed onto a three-dimensional article, such as a tray or mat.

UK UNREGISTERED DESIGN RIGHT

It has been recognised in the UK that industry does not make enough use of the design registration system and that the actual process of registration is in itself quite cumbersome, let alone costly, although not nearly as costly as taking out patents.

There has also been a problem in applying the law of copyright to three-dimensional designs. This has been addressed by legislation in 1988 which introduced an 'Unregistered Design Right' (UDR or Design Right for short). This is a new Intellectual Property Right.

UK UNREGISTERED DESIGN RIGHTS: A SUMMARY

- It is not really a full monopoly right, it only prevents against copying.

- It only lasts for ten years running from the date of first marketing in the UK of a product with the design, subject to a maximum of fifteen years from creation of the design.

- Exclusive rights are only granted for the first five years, rights for the remaining five years are 'non-exclusive', i.e. anyone is entitled to obtain a licence on reasonable terms from the owner of the UDR.

- It does not apply to two-dimensional designs.

- It does apply to completely functional designs, i.e. there is no requirement of aesthetic quality, but commonplace designs are not covered.

- Spare parts manufacturers are given a dispensation by virtue of the so-called 'must fit' and 'must match' designs, which cannot be protected by UDR.

- It applies to designs created by any national, resident or company in the EU, insofar as these are marketed in the territory of the UK.

REMEMBER

DO:

- Make sure you have a standard assignment or employment contract where employees assign their copyright to your company.

- Use the copyright symbol ©, and place it prominently on all your company's copyright material.

- Consider the benefits of design registration, which is relatively inexpensive, for designs with genuine aesthetic appeal.

- Know that design registration is the only form of monopoly right for industrial designs – you do not have to prove a competitor has actually copied your design.

- Be aware of the fall-back, automatic protection given in the UK by unregistered design rights.

DO NOT:

- Assume copyright covers ideas and concepts – it doesn't; it only protects against copying of actual expressions (e.g. on paper) of ideas and concepts.

- Confuse copyright and patents – patents give you a monopoly right that may be very hard to get around; copyright does not.

- Copy other people's material; this is the one sure way to know you are not infringing anyone else's copyright.

- Put a product with a new design on the market before you have applied for design registration.

Chapter 8

How To Manage Your Patent And Trade Mark Portfolio, And Make Money From It

This chapter will help you to:
- manage your intellectual property portfolio.

How To Manage Your Patent And Trade Mark Portfolio, And Make Money From It

> Money talks, they say. All it ever said to me was 'goodbye'.
>
> Cary Grant

Your intellectual property rights, i.e. your granted patents, registered designs and registered trade marks, are very valuable assets for your company. These make up a portfolio, which must be maintained and managed.

The State has granted you these exclusive rights, but it will not police them for you. You as owner of this property must be vigilant, constantly on the watch for infringers and imitators, and be prepared to take action against them.

MAINTAINING RIGHTS IN FORCE: RENEWAL FEES

A patent can be maintained in force for twenty years, whereupon your monopoly rights expire, and anyone is then free to use the patented invention. An annual renewal fee must be paid on each patent to the Patent Office, although the first two years are free in Ireland and the first four years are free in the UK.

There is a sliding scale with the first renewal fee being about £100, rising to about £500 in the final year. This is similar in other countries, but the cost of maintaining a significant portfolio of patents, with separate annual renewal fees being paid in each country, and which can be counted on to increase year on year, is clearly a significant item.

If a patent is not renewed on time, it will lapse, and legal rights will lapse after six months grace for late payment of fees. After that, it can be very difficult indeed to bring a lapsed patent back to life and so every care should be taken to have a proper system in place.

- A registered design can be maintained for fifteen years in Ireland and 25 years in the UK on payment of renewal fees every five years.

- A registered trade mark is the best of all, as it can be maintained indefinitely, on payment of a renewal fee every ten years.

- There are no renewal fees for copyright or unregistered design right (UK).

Responsibility can be given to your patent attorney to actually pay renewal fees, or there are even some firms specialising in renewals of patents, designs and trade marks. But you must set up a proper renewal system in your company to give timely instructions to the fee payment service.

TYPE OF PROTECTION	MAXIMUM TERM	RENEW
Patent	20 years	Every year
Registered Design (Ireland)	15 years	Every 5 years
Registered Design (UK)	25 years	Every 5 years
Registered Trade Mark	Indefinite	Every 10 years
Copyright	70 years +	Never
Unregistered Design (UK)	10 years	Never

ABUSE OF MONOPOLY RIGHTS AND COMPULSORY LICENCES

If you are slow to exploit your patent monopoly, e.g. if the patented product requires further development work, does not reach the market for several years after a patent is granted or the quantity manufactured does not even meet domestic demand, there may be an abuse of monopoly rights. If you simply maintain the patent in force with no intention of ever bringing the patented product to market, then there is certainly an abuse of monopoly rights. You cannot play dog in the manger.

To counter this, there is a provision in patent law for what is called 'compulsory' licensing. This is where, after a period of three years from the grant of the patent, a third party can apply, through the Patent Office or the courts, for a licence to make and sell the patented products, and you, as the patent holder must grant a licence on reasonable terms if there is an evident abuse of your monopoly rights. You will of course receive the royalty income, but this is not a good situation because you will not be able to choose your licensees, who will of course be competing with you.

LICENCES AS OF RIGHT

Another situation exists where you may be thinking of letting a patent lapse if you have no plans to exploit that technology. Instead of letting the patent lapse, you can inform the Patent Office that you are prepared to grant a licence to anyone who asks for one, on reasonable terms. Once you do this, the annual renewal fees are immediately halved for the remainder of the patent term as a concession, a substantial saving in costs.

NON-USE OF REGISTERED TRADE MARKS

You do not actually have to be using a trade mark to have it registered, i.e. it is possible to apply for registration based on your intention to use the trade mark in the future. However, once registered, if the trade mark has not been used in commerce in connection with the goods or services in question after a period of five years, a third party may apply to have it removed from the Trade Marks Register.

It is very important therefore to ensure that the trade marks you are actually using in the market-place correspond exactly with the trade marks as registered, or else you could find that you have no protection at all. If you have a brand image, which is re-vamped, the new brand may contain trade marks including different elements or logos that may have to be registered again. Brands, and brand images, evolve all the time, and so the process of registering trade marks is one that does not stop after the original brand name was first conjured up.

MARKING OF PRODUCTS

Patents: Product Marking

When you have applied for a patent, you should make the most of the deterrent value of this by putting the words 'patents pending' on the product packaging and literature. Once granted, you should put the word 'patent' followed by the serial number of the granted patent, or patents, which relate to that product or the process by which it is made. Mark it clearly on the packaging or the product itself.

Failure to include the patent number could result in an infringer using the defence of 'innocent infringement', i.e. by claiming that he was not aware that a patent existed. If the infringer was successful with this defence, infringement would have to stop, as a court would award an injunction, but you would not be able to get them to pay over monetary compensation.

Designs: Product Marking

Likewise, if a design is registered, 'registered design' (or 'reg. des.') followed by the serial number, should be marked on the relevant products for the same reason.

Trade Marks: Product Marking

If you are using a trade mark, regardless of whether or not it is registered, you should use the superscript symbol ™, or ^{SM} if it is a service mark.

If it is registered, you are entitled to use the symbol ®, but strictly speaking this should not be used if the goods are going to be exported to countries where there is no registration. In most countries, the use of the symbol ® to denote a registered trade mark, where there is in fact no registration, is an offence. In the USA, it will only be possible to obtain monetary compensation in an infringement action if the symbol ® has been used.

> **WORD TO THE WISE**
> The valuable rights which are acquired by registration of your trade mark can be lost if a trade mark is not used correctly or if you allow careless usage.

Keep Relevance of Marking Under Review

It is also wrong, and it is an offence, to make any claim that a patent exists on a product, when it does not, or equally, when it has lapsed. It is not uncommon to see a patent marking on a product which really should not be there anymore.

All of these markings for patent, designs and trade marks should be reviewed along with other product packaging information on a regular basis.

CORRECT USAGE OF REGISTERED TRADE MARKS

Genericide

The valuable rights, which are acquired by registration of your trade mark, can be lost if a trade mark is not used correctly or if you allow careless usage. You may think it something of an accolade for your product to be known generically by your trade mark, but that is dangerous because customers will soon become happy to receive your competitors goods when asked for by using your trade mark in a generic sense.

The value of your trade mark will soon become so diluted that eventually it will serve no purpose at all to distinguish your goods from your competitors. Americans call it 'genericide'. Many trade marks have died this death and are now words in everyday use, such as gramophone, aspirin, zip, tabloid and escalator. Then there are others, which while still registered trade marks, are in danger or in their death throes because they are frequently thought of by the public as being common names, e.g. *Biro, Hoover, Thermos* and *Cellophane*.

Some hard work is required by the owner of the latter trade marks to keep them alive and validly registered. This includes vigilance and an *insistence* by the trade mark owner that there is always a correct usage of the trade marks in a proper trade mark sense, in advertising, in print, on packaging, etc.

FIVE RULES FOR CORRECT TRADE MARK USAGE

Rule 1 **Always use a trade mark as an adjective.**
A trade mark is an adjective, not a noun or a verb, but may be used carelessly in that way in advertising. For example, always refer to 'a Hoover vacuum cleaner' and not 'hoovering' and 'a Hoover'.

Rule 2 **Do not use plurals or possessives.** A trade mark must not appear in the plural or in a possessive sense. For example, it is bad to say 'Biros' but correct to say 'Biro pens' and 'Bic's new razor' should be 'the new Bic razor'.

Rule 3 **Always use a trade mark with a generic term.** A trade mark must always be used in print next to or close to a generic word or phrase that describes the product, e.g. 'Thermos, the original vacuum flask'.

Rule 4 **Indicate a trade mark clearly in print.** There are numerous ways of indicating that a word is a trade mark, to give it distinctive treatment in print. The first letter should always be capitalised, but the following are acceptable: quotation marks (e.g. 'Velux' attic windows); capital letters (e.g. GUINNESS stout); italics (e.g. *Penguin* paperbacks); bold type (e.g. **Hamlet** cigars); or by using a superscript symbol (e.g. ® or ™).

Rule 5 **Use the word 'registered'.** Always use a footnote in print or on packaging to denote that "XYZ is a registered trade mark of ABC Ltd" as well as using the symbol ® to indicate that a word or device is a trade mark which is registered.

POLICING YOUR COMPANY'S PATENT AND TRADE MARK PORTFOLIO

Use your Sales Force

Everyone in your company must be aware of your patent and trade mark portfolio and report any apparent threat from competitors. Your sales force should be constantly on the look out for competitor activity.

If you become aware of a similar trade mark, or similar-sounding trade mark, even if this is for a different product, it is safer to bring this to the attention of your trade mark adviser. For a large international trade mark portfolio, watching services are available to ensure that no competitor attempts to register your trade mark, or a similar-sounding trade mark, in another country. Your trade mark agent should advise you how to set up these watches.

> **WORD TO THE WISE**
> Everyone in your company must be aware of your patent and trade mark portfolio and should report any apparent threat from competitors.

Use your Distributors

Make sure your network of distributors and agents also bring to your attention any possible infringing activity. It is practically impossible for any small to medium-sized company to police its patents or spend substantial time at this, but if a potential infringing activity is brought to your attention, you should get advice immediately.

If you do nothing, the problem could grow, and delay in bringing the matter to court, if that is what has to be done, could possibly ruin your chances of a successful outcome. The infringer could say in his defence that if you did nothing after all this time, that you must surely have condoned his activity.

Use a Watching Service

A watching search can also be set up for patents (see Chapter 5) which will alert you quickly to other parties who may, innocently or otherwise, have recently filed a patent application covering a product similar to your patented product.

MAKING MONEY FROM YOUR PATENT PORTFOLIO: LICENSING OUT

If a company has developed a patented technology, and wants to penetrate export markets quickly, it may be possible to license out the technology if a patent has been obtained in the relevant country so generating an income stream from licence royalties. It may make much more sense to locate a partner in another country under a manufacturing and/or sales licence agreement to serve that market.

The related know-how and technical expertise which you have developed could all be included in a technology transfer agreement, as well as licensing the use of your trade mark, if it is appropriate in the country concerned. Really, licensing out your patented technology is the ultimate way to make money from your patent portfolio. This especially makes sense for a small company without an international marketing structure and which has not yet developed supply and distribution chains. A licensing deal can be set up relatively quickly and government agencies and licensing consultants are there to help you identify suitable prospective partners and to negotiate the whole deal.

HOW TO SAVE MONEY BY LICENSING IN

Technology transfer is a two-way process. Rather than developing its own new products and technologies, a smaller company can 'buy in' a proved and tested technology by entering into a licence with an outside party which already holds a patent. Compare this with the cost of personnel who you have hired or contracted to carry out research and design work, and the uncertainty of whether new products can be brought online, within budget and on time.

The cost of buying into a licence arrangement will

normally involve an up-front payment to the patent holder and then continuing royalty payments. In Ireland, very substantial government grants exist to cover licence downpayments and associated costs but these grants are underutilised.

A licensing consultant, or the industrial development agencies, could help a company identify inward licensing opportunities and make the right connections. A patent attorney could assess the value of the patent and whether it is worth the money. Unfortunately many companies are suspicious of this strategy: if we have not invented it, then it cannot be any good. On the other hand, very many successful technology transfer agreements are in place, both sides deriving enormous benefits from a licensing strategy, whether this is licensing out or licensing in.

Exclusive Licence

The best kind of patent licence agreement is an exclusive manufacturing and sales licence. This means that the company to whom the licence has been granted has the full force of the patent behind it, and even the patent holder is not entitled to compete with you in the licensed territory. It is as if the company has acquired the patent for that territory.

Sole Licence

A sole licence is one where the company to whom the licence has been granted and the patent holder can both exploit the patent in that territory together to the exclusion of everyone else.

Non-exclusive Licence

A non-exclusive licence is one that is not so good, because the patent holder can also compete with you, and is free to grant other non-exclusive licences to other competitors in your territory.

Always get Advice before Finalising a Licence

In all cases a well-drafted licence agreement will be required and its terms will be open to negotiation, in particular the royalty terms and the manner in which the royalties are paid. A patent attorney or solicitor should review the terms of any licence agreement before it is signed.

Any licence agreement must not contain terms that fall foul of EU Competition Rules and may be completely invalid if it does. This is yet another reason for having the fine print of any licence agreement reviewed thoroughly by your professional advisors.

ROYALTIES

The most crucial terms in any licence agreement involving patented processes or technology are those relating to royalties. How much will you make if you are licensing out? How much will you pay if you are licensing in? Royalties can be calculated in different ways, for example:

- as an agreed sum per unit of production, e.g. £x per unit. This could be indexed to allow for price or money value fluctuations;
- as an agreed proportion of the unit price, e.g. x per cent of ex-works price, or net-selling price (sales price less discounts and tax);
- as an agreed sum made annually or in instalments;
- on a sliding scale, decreasing at certain production thresholds as volume increases;
- any combination of the above.

FACTORS INFLUENCING ACTUAL ROYALTY RATES

1. A rate of 1 per cent of net selling price would generally be considered to be rather low, 10 per cent

may be an average rate, while 15 per cent would be high, in most fields of technology. A rule of thumb is to commence negotiations at a figure that is approximately 25 per cent of the net profit margin.

2. Unit cost versus expected sales volume, i.e. low unit cost/high sales volume indicates a low rate while high unit cost/low sales volume indicates a higher rate. In the case of a patented machine, it would be preferable to base royalties on the value of products made by the machine (normally also covered by the patent) if sales of the actual machine itself were limited.

3. Since the projection of expected sales may be uncertain, a royalty scale could be agreed with a diminishing royalty rate proportional to increasing sales, e.g. if sales were expected to be low in the first year, a higher royalty could be demanded, with a lower royalty in the following year when sales increase.

4. The overall investment in research and development must be taken into account in valuing a product or technology to be licensed. When this is very high, e.g. in the case of the pharmaceutical industry, a royalty as high as 30-50 per cent may be justified.

5. In general an exclusive licence or a sole licence will demand a higher royalty than a non-exclusive licence.

6. In general the more advantageous the other terms of the whole agreement, for example if the agreement also includes the transfer of related know-how, the more justification there is for a higher royalty.

7. Last but not least, it must be remembered that the royalty finally agreed upon will depend to a large extent on what the company taking the licence is prepared to pay.

An exclusive licence generally includes a minimum royalty provision, i.e. royalty payments must reach a minimum annual level. If this is not reached, the patent holder may be entitled to terminate the licence or require that the shortfall be made up by a lump sum payment.

TAX TREATMENT OF LICENCE ROYALTIES

An Irish company, or individual resident in Ireland for tax purposes, will in certain circumstances be entitled to 100 per cent tax exemption on patent royalty income. This is indeed an incentive for Irish companies to license out their patented technology. Advice from a tax consultant must be sought. The patented invention must have been made and developed in Ireland, and must relate to a manufactured product, but other conditions apply which are complex and subject to change.

REMEMBER

DO:

- Set up a proper renewal system in your company.

- Mark each product to indicate clearly that it is patented, or that it is 'patents pending', that there is a registered design or that a trade mark is registered.

- Insist on the correct usage of your trade marks to ensure that they don't become the common name or generic name of a product – that will be the death of your trade mark.

- Be aware that it is your responsibility to police your patents and trade marks and the activities of imitators.

- Exploit your patents by searching for licensing out opportunities, a lot of money can be made from patent royalties.

DO NOT:

- Allow very valuable legal rights given by patents and registered trade marks to lapse by simple non-payment of renewal fees.

- Sit on a patent and not exploit it; this is an abuse of monopoly rights and you will be vulnerable to compulsory licensing to third parties.

- Leave a patent number marked on a product if the patent has expired or use the symbol ® if a trade mark is not a registered trade mark.

- Allow any infringers to get away with it; get advice immediately from a patent attorney.

- Reinvent the wheel – search out licensing in opportunities; the cost of royalty payments could be much less than developing your own technology – a tried and tested one may already be out there.

Chapter 9

How To Enforce Your Rights, Deal With Problems Caused By Your Competitors' Rights And Avoid Losing A Lot Of Money

This chapter will help you to:

- deal with enforcement issues.

How To Enforce Your Rights, Deal With Problems Caused By Your Competitors' Rights And Avoid Losing A Lot Of Money

> Knowledge is the treasure, but judgement is the treasurer of a wise man.
>
> William Penn

When a patented invention is truly successful, i.e. when the patented technology gives your company a real competitive edge, you can be certain of one thing: attempts will be made to copy your product. Imitation may be seen as flattery, but you will have to do something about it, and this means being prepared to enforce your patent quickly, the value of your registered trade marks and carefully established brands will be diminished quickly. For the small to medium-sized company, the prospect of defending your legal rights in court can be daunting, especially where your case is not clear-cut.

WHEN IS A PATENT INFRINGED?

Patent 'Claims' Define the Scope of Protection

At the end of every patent document, there is a set of patent 'claims'. These claims define very precisely all the *essential* features of the patented invention. These features are always described in very generalised terminology, such as 'means for' performing a particular function, which could be realised in any number of different ways. A patent is only infringed when the infringer has replicated each and every one of these essential features. If the

claims have not been well drafted, or contain loop-
holes, there may be a way for the infringer to 'get
around' the patent, but the court will be the final
arbiter on what the patent covers and what it does
not.

The Court's Interpretation is what Matters

The way in which patent claims are interpreted is
governed to some extent by case law, which goes
back quite a long way. Courts generally tend to
come down in favour of the patent holder. While a
precise definition of the scope of the invention must
be given in the patent claims, there have been cases
where the courts have not tied the patent holder to
a very literal interpretation of his patent claims, and
an infringer has still been caught by adopting some
'mechanical equivalent' or very obviously equivalent
feature even though that is not specified in the
claims of the patent.

As soon as you become aware of any possible
infringement of your patent, or if you discover a
patent which you believe your company may be
infringing, you should immediately seek a patent
attorney's advice. Get a patent attorney's opinion,
but remember that it may be difficult to obtain a
definite opinion because in the end a court has to
decide whether or not a patent is infringed.

WHAT IS INVOLVED IN ENFORCING A PATENT?

Step 1:   Issue a Warning Letter

If you decide to proceed with a legal action against
an infringer, whether of a patent or a registered
trade mark, the first step is to have your patent
attorney or solicitor issue a warning letter. Do not
send this letter yourself. A warning letter has to be
drafted very carefully.

This applies in particular to letters addressed to distributors, retailers, importers or customers, anyone who is not a primary producer of the allegedly infringing product, because such a person would be entitled to bring a counteraction against you for issuing an unjustified threat of a patent infringement action. In other words, there are circumstances where you may not have as good a case as you think and a warning letter could backfire, causing you to be liable to damages caused to the supposed infringer.

Step 2: Issue Proceedings

The warning letter usually sets a term for reply, and if there is no reply, you could proceed to issue legal proceedings through your solicitor.

A date for a preliminary court hearing could be set relatively quickly, i.e. within months, not years, where your legal advisors would be seeking to obtain an interim or 'interlocutory' injunction against the infringer, to prevent further infringement from taking place until a full hearing or trial of the infringement action is appointed.

Step 3: Do a Deal or Seek an Interim Injunction

Interlocutory proceedings involve the appointment of a patent attorney, a solicitor and a barrister. This is going to be expensive, and in a patent case will probably cost up to £10,000. The idea would be either to extract a written undertaking from the infringer to cease the infringement or negotiate a settlement, *before* any court hearing, with the consequential costs. If you are successful and obtain an interim injunction, you should be able to recover some of the legal costs, as may be determined by the court.

Step 4:   Interlocutory Proceedings

In deciding whether or not to grant an injunction,

which of course will put an end to the infringer's activities, the court has to balance carefully whether or not the status quo should be allowed to continue until a full trial, and whether the loss suffered by the patent holder will be adequately compensated by monetary damages awarded later. Also if the patent holder has delayed instituting proceedings long after he first knew of the infringement, an interim injunction is unlikely to be granted.

Step 5:   Contested Case and Full Trial

An interim injunction, assuming it is granted, is nearly always the end of the matter. In some cases, the alleged infringer will contest the case and eventually there will be a full trial of the action, which could go on for many days or weeks in court, involving very substantial legal costs.

DEFENCES TO AN INFRINGEMENT ACTION

Deny Infringement

The alleged infringer will obviously deny infringement and their argument will be that what they were doing, or the product they were selling, does not fall within the terms of the patent claims. The court will therefore have to decide precisely what is covered by the patent.

Patent is Invalid

The alleged infringer can try to build a case that the patent is not valid, should not have been granted at all and therefore cannot be enforced against them. The issue of the validity of the patent can only be considered at the full trial and involves delving into the 'prior art', i.e. the sum total of the published literature and what was known to a person who would be 'skilled in the art' before the earliest date or priority date of the patent. Expert witnesses and technical experts can be called and crossexamined.

We did not Know there was a Patent

The alleged infringer can claim that they are innocent because they did not know there was a patent. If your product or packaging does not include a marking that includes the word 'patent' or 'patented' and the patent number, this defence can be successful, but only to the extent that the infringer may escape having to pay the patent holder monetary damages. The court would still award an injunction to stop the infringements.

> **WORD TO THE WISE**
> Trade mark litigation is more common and usually less expensive than litigation involving patents.

MONETARY DAMAGES

If you are successful and win a patent infringement action, you would be entitled to be awarded a sum of money by the court to be paid by the infringer for the damage caused. This could be based on profits made by the infringer, or profits lost by the patent holder, or the amount of money which the patent holder would have made if the infringer had been paying licence royalties.

In a copyright case, 'conversion damages' may be awarded, which are more generous, amounting to the full value of the infringing articles. The infringer may also be ordered to surrender all stocks in hand of the infringing articles or these may be destroyed.

If past infringements have been going on for a long time, it may be difficult to recover damages. The infringer might claim 'implied licence', i.e. that if the patent holder delayed bringing the action for some years, then during that time he must surely have condoned the infringement. Also there is the six year statute of limitations rule.

TRADE MARK LITIGATION

This is more common and generally much less expensive than any litigation involving patents. The issues are generally more straightforward and take up less court time. If it can be shown that the registered proprietor has not used a trade mark for a period of five years on the relevant goods, the registered trade mark could be 'cancelled' or struck off from the Trade Marks Register.

Remember a trade mark is registered for certain goods and services which are specified in the registration, and it would be vulnerable to attack if it is not used, more or less continuously, for all those goods and services.

In a trade mark action, it would be a defence that the registered proprietor no longer owns the trade mark rights. In other words, if a company is involved in a takeover or merger, or assigns its trade mark rights to another company, this must all be recorded in the Trade Marks Register by your trade mark agent and before any litigation is started. The *Registered Proprietor* is the company whose name is recorded as such in the official Trade Mark Register at the Patent Office.

There can be a quite considerable cost involved in recording such changes for an international portfolio of trade marks, registered in many countries.

PASSING OFF

Even if your trade mark has not been registered, it is still possible to bring an action against anyone who imitates your brand, trade mark or packaging in a way which may mislead consumers as 'passing off' their goods as your goods. This is more complicated than a straightforward action involving a registered trade mark, because it is necessary to establish that you have a genuine reputation and that the actions of the imitator have been calculated to, and have in fact, cashed in on your reputation and goodwill.

You have to establish that you have some common law right to your (unregistered) trade mark. This is always open to argument and will involve more time in court and will be more expensive.

This is one very good reason for registering your trade marks, because registration gives you statutory rights and you do not have to first establish that you have a legal right as in a passing-off action.

> **WORD TO THE WISE**
> Before you ever get involved in any form of litigation, remember that above all else it takes up an enormous amount of time and involves stress. All of this represents a lost opportunity cost that can never be recovered, even if you are victorious. It is all time and effort that could be better spent on more productive endeavour.

AVOID LITIGATION AT ALL COSTS

A full patent infringement action going to trial could expose you to a potential six or seven figure liability, if you lose. If you are on the winning side, the court may award legal costs and monetary damages to recompense you for damage caused by the infringer, but the costs awarded are unlikely to cover all your legal costs, and the monetary damages are not exactly generous. The calculation of damages is set down by statue, and is not at the court's discretion. Financial reward is, therefore, not a good motive for starting a legal action.

If you are on the losing side, you may have to pay the winning side's legal costs and it is you who will have to pay the monetary damages awarded by the court.

Absolutely never get involved in any litigation involving a US patent as this could mean financial ruin. The legal costs are horrendous and US courts can award punitive damages (three times the normal award) if the infringer can be shown to have known that the patent existed but nevertheless went ahead and infringed.

The threat of legal proceedings, and even going to the stage of applying for an interlocutory injunction in a patent case, can often force a settlement and this is the outcome everyone wants. It may be possible to seek a remedy

> **WORD TO THE WISE**
> A full patent infringement action going to trial could expose you to a potential six or seven figure liability – if you lose.

through a lower court, such as the Irish District Court or UK County Court, where costs are lower, but so are the damages that may be awarded. Generally, a patent action will involve proceedings in a higher court, the Irish High Court or UK Patents Court where you must appoint a barrister and there is no way of saving costs.

ALTERNATIVE DISPUTE RESOLUTION

You could avoid going to court altogether if both sides are willing to submit to independent arbitration. An international system now exists with rules laid down by the World Intellectual Property Office, a UN body, based in Geneva. It is a relatively new process, but costs are likely to be less than full court proceedings, with the advantage that all hearings are in private and the outcome is not publicly known.

PATENT INSURANCE

For the small or medium-sized company which is serious about enforcing its patents, but cannot possibly suffer the exposure to the enormous financial liability which litigation involves, it is possible to take out patent insurance. This will cover you for legal costs and for the cost of defending the legal action.

However, the small print of the policy may require that you obtain a legal opinion that your patent is valid and enforceable before making a claim, but that opinion may be impossible to obtain before the court has made a decision. You should beware of patent insurance policies were the premium costs a few hundred pounds, because these will probably never pay out. The premium for really serious cover will probably cost you several thousand pounds a year, but this may well be worth it if you have an important patent that you mean to enforce.

HOW TO DEAL WITH PROBLEMS CAUSED BY YOUR COMPETITORS' RIGHTS

Threatening Letters

If you are at the receiving end of a threatening letter, seek immediate advice from a patent attorney or trade mark agent. He/she will immediately assess the situation, and if there is no conflict of interests will advise you as to the scope of the patent or trade mark registration and if you really are likely to infringe.

Prior User Rights

If you have sold a product or used a process covered by the patent *before* the earliest date or priority date of the patent, then there can be no infringement. If the product was previously on sale, then a patent should not have been granted because the invention was clearly not new.

If you had been using the process secretly before the relevant date, the patent may still stand up, but you would have a 'prior user right' which would allow you to continue using your process as you have always done, without any liability for patent infringement.

Patent Holder may have a Weak Patent

You can be lucky and find that the threatening letter may not really be a problem after all. Your patent attorney may be able to unearth some fairly obscure prior art document which was not located by the Patent Office when it did its own searches, which could be used as ammunition to attack the validity of the patent.

The patent may therefore be weaker than the patent holder thinks, and they may be put off trying to enforce it. However, a strong patent not open to any worthwhile attack on its validity, is a very formidable weapon. You may just have to be prepared to sit down, negotiate a deal and pay a royalty.

Is the Patent in Force?

It is fairly obvious, but nevertheless worth checking if the patent in question is actually in force and that renewal fees have been paid. For a European patent, it may not have been maintained in force in *all* the countries listed as 'designated countries' on the front page of the granted European patent. An application to restore a lapsed patent can be opposed by a third party.

REMEMBER

DO:

- Find out how much potential liability you have in any litigation, if you might be on the losing side; this will help you think in terms of a deal!

- Act quickly if you are serious about enforcing your legal rights; delays could affect your chances of being granted on interim injunction.

- Realise that the threat of legal proceedings may bring the matter to a head; always be prepared to negotiate.

- Be careful to record all changes of ownership of patents and registered trade marks – generally only the registered owner can sue.

- Consider the enormous amount of time you will spend if you are involved in litigation; this is an invisible cost.

DO NOT:

- Ever get involved in any form of litigation if there is a way out or a way to avoid it.

- Ever send a warning letter to a suspected infringer without a patent attorney's advice; such letters have to be carefully worded.

- Ignore other people's patents; get advice as to whether or not you infringe or whether the patent is in force and what your liabilities are.

- Take out patent insurance unless it gives serious cover against litigation costs.

- Start legal action to extract money from a competitor – financial gain is not a good motive.

Further Resources

- Lists of professional representatives and information.
- Useful internet websites.
- Licensing consultants.

Further Resources

LISTS OF PROFESSIONAL REPRESENTATIVES AND INFORMATION

A List of European Patent Attorneys may be obtained from the following Institutions

The European Patent Office
27 Erhardtstrasse
D-80298 Munich
Germany
Tel: 0049 89 2399-0
Fax: 0049 89 2399 4465

Free publications include:
European Patents
What is Patentable?
How to get a European Patent

The European Patent Institute
Postfach 26 01 12
D-80058 Munich
Germany
Tel: 0049 89 201 7080
Fax: 0049 89 202 1548

Free publications include:
An Introduction to Patents in Europe

A List of Community Trade Mark Attorneys may be obtained from the following Insitution

Office for the Harmonisation of the Internal Market (Trade Marks & Designs)
Avda. De Aguilera, 20
03006 Alicante
Spain
Tel: 0034 96 513 9100
Fax: 0034 96 513 9173

Subscriber publications include:
Community Trade Marks Journal

A List of UK Chartered Patent Agents may be obtained from the following Institution

The Chartered Institute of Patent Agents
Staple Inn Buildings
High Holborn
London WC1V 7PZ
UK
Tel: (0044/0) 171 405 9450
Fax: (0044/0) 171 430 0471

A List of UK Trade Mark Agents may be obtained from the following Institution

The Institute of Trade Mark Agents
Canterbury House
2-6 Sydenham Road
Croydon
Surrey CR0 9XE
UK
Tel: (0044/0) 181 686 2052
Fax: (0044/0) 181 680 5723

A List of Irish Patent Agents and Trade Mark Agents may be obtained from the following Institutions

The Patents Office
Government Buildings
Hebron Road
Kilkenny
Ireland
Tel: (00353/0) 56 20 111
Fax: (00353/0) 56 20 100

Free publications include:
General Information on Patents for Inventions

The Secretary
The Association of Patent and Trade Mark Agents
c/o 27 Clyde Road
Dublin 4
Ireland
Tel: (00353/0) 1 660 2111
Fax: (00353/0) 1 668 2844

A Comprehensive Information Pack on UK Patents, Designs, Trade Marks and Copyright is available from the following Institution

The Patent Office
Concept House
Cardiff Road
Newport
South Wales NP9 1RH
UK
Tel: (0044/0) 1633 813 585
Fax: (0044/0) 1633 814 444

Information is available from the World Intellectual Property Organisation in Geneva

WIPO
34 Chemin des Colombettes
CH-1211 Geneva 20
Switzerland
Tel: 00 41 22 730 9111
Fax: 00 41 22 733 5428

Information includes:

International Classification of Trade Marks, Service Marks

International Classification of Designs

International Patent Classification (IPC) Catchword Index

WIPO – General Information

PCT Applicants Guide

USEFUL INTERNET WEBSITES

Patent documents, Patent Offices, General Information

www.patent.gov.uk	British Patent Office
www.european-patent-office.org	European Patent Office
www.uspto.gov	US Patent and Trademark Office
www.patent.womplex.ibm.com	IBM Patent Server (Patent Documents)
www.jpo-miti.jp	Japanese Patent Office

www.wipo.int   World
                                Intellectual
                                Property
                                Organisation

Links to Patent Attorney Sites

www.cipa.org.uk/cipa/index.html Chartered
                                 Institute of
                                 Patent Agents
www.piperpat.co.nz/world.html#areas New Zealand firm
                                 with global links

LICENSING CONSULTANTS

A list may be obtained from the following institutions

The Licensing Executives Society (Britain & Ireland)
c/o MEDTAP International
27 Gilbert Street
London W1Y 1RL
UK
Attn   Ms Renate Siebrasse, Administrator
Tel: (0044/0) 171 290 9400
Fax: (0044/0) 171 629 9705
e-mail: renate@tmckew.demon.co.uk